Wild G
big book *of*
liturgies

Wild Goose
big book *of*
liturgies

wild goose
publications
www.**ionabooks**.com

Published 2017, reprinted 2018
Wild Goose Publications
21 Carlton Court, Glasgow G5 9JP, UK,
the publishing division of the Iona Community.
Scottish Charity No. SC003794. Limited Company Reg. No. SC096243.

ISBN 978-1-84952-541-1

Cover photo © Lostbear | Dreamstime.com

Overseas distribution
Australia: Willow Connection Pty Ltd, Unit 4A, 3–9 Kenneth Road,
Manly Vale, NSW 2093
New Zealand: Pleroma, Higginson Street, Otane 4170, Central Hawkes Bay
Canada: Bayard Distribution, 10 Lower Spadina Ave., Suite 400, Toronto,
Ontario M5V 2Z

Printed by Bell & Bain, Thornliebank, Glasgow

Contents

A wee word for Advent

John Harvey

Opening words:

In the beginning, when it was very dark, God said: 'Let there be light',
AND THERE WAS LIGHT.
God's light goes on shining in the darkness
AND THE DARKNESS HAS NEVER PUT IT OUT.

Bible reading (Matthew 5:14–16):

Jesus said: 'You are like light for the whole world. A city built on a hill cannot be hidden. No one lights a candle and puts it under a bowl; instead, they put it on a candlestick, where it gives light all around. In the same way, your light must shine before others, so that they will see the good things that you do, and praise God in heaven.'

Prayers:

Light a candle/tea-light between each prayer of concern.

We remember people whose lives have had a lot of darkness in them ...

God, in your mercy,
HEAR OUR PRAYER.

We thank God for the people whose lives have been like light in dark places ...

God, in your mercy,
HEAR OUR PRAYER.

We pray for ourselves, that God's light may shine in us ...

God, in your mercy,
HEAR OUR PRAYER.

Song: 'Shine a light', by Brian Woodcock

Shine a light

Words and music by Brian Woodcock

Shine a light! Shine a light!
Shine a light for the prophets of the world.
Shine a light for the beacons that burn in every age
    till his kingdom come
    and his will is done
    and the glory of the Lord is revealed.

Shine another! Shine another!
Shine a light in the darkness of the world.
It's for John the Baptist, and those who pave the way
    till his kingdom come …

Shine another light! Shine another light!
Shine a light at the heart of all the world.
And the third is for Mary, and all that gives him birth
    till his kingdom come …

Shine a dozen lights! Shine a thousand lights!
Let them shine from the hilltops of the world.
They're for you; they're for me;
they're for all who wait for him
    till his kingdom come …

Come into the light! Come into the light!
Jesus Christ is the light of all the world.
And his day has arrived, and the darkness is no more,
    for his kingdom's come
    and his will is done
    and the glory of the Lord is revealed.

(Song by Brian Woodcock)

Closing words:

The light of God
TO LEAD US AND MAKE US UNAFRAID.

The power of God
TO PROTECT US AND MAKE US STRONG.

The joy of God
TO HEAL US AND MAKE US HAPPY.

The grace of God
TO BLESS US AND KEEP US LOVING,
NOW AND EVERMORE. AMEN

God's family first
All-age worship for
the first Sunday of Advent

Nancy Cocks

Include children and young people, using several voices alongside the Leader's.

Talking about Advent:

Worship leader (conversationally):

December is a month of candles.

When do we often have candles? ...

    – birthdays

    – when the power goes out and we're left in the dark

    – dinner parties ...

Birthday candles: one more each year, so our cake gets brighter every year. December is a month for candles in church – we light one candle this week, next week we'll light two, and so on. So just like a birthday cake gets brighter when more candles are burning, our Advent wreath will get brighter and brighter this month just as the December days get darker because the sun shines for the fewest hours.

We're also celebrating something important – an important birthday ...

We're getting ready to celebrate Jesus' birthday.

And for people who follow Jesus, he is 'the Light of the world' – the one who shines the light of God's love into our darkest times: to warm our hearts like a candle flame and help us find our way, like a candle helps us when the electricity goes out.

So this is our month for candles – to feel the light of God's love growing brighter.

And this is our month to shine like a candle – to let God's love shine for others through our lives.

So I've got a candle for each of you to let your little light shine.

Give a small battery-operated candle to each child ...

We light the candles of Advent – the candle of hope:

Here you could use a candle-lighting liturgy from your Church, or one of the candle-lighting liturgies in Candles and Conifers, *Ruth Burgess, Wild Goose Publications.*

Song: 'O come, O come Emmanuel (verses 1, 6, 7)

Bible reading: We hear a word from Isaiah (Isaiah 9)

Voice one: The people who walked in darkness have seen a great light.

Voice two: Those who lived in a land of deep darkness – on them light has shined.

Voice one: For a child has been born for us, a son given to us.

Voice two: Authority rests upon his shoulders; and he is named Wonderful Counsellor, Mighty God, Everlasting Father, Prince of Peace.

Voice one: His rule shall grow continually, and there shall be endless peace for his kingdom.

We say sorry to God:

Dear God, our love for you is like a candle flame. When things are calm, our love shines brightly. But when we get worried, our love flickers. When things go wrong, it feels like we're walking in deep darkness. God, forgive us when our love for you dies away like a candle that's burned down. Fill us with your love so that our love burns more brightly in Jesus' name. Amen

We hear a word from Jesus:

Remember, Jesus said, *'I am the light of the world. Whoever follows me will never walk in darkness but will have the light of life.'* When we say sorry to God from the bottom of our hearts, Jesus will light up our lives with his love. So we can sing:

Song: 'This little light of mine' (in various songbooks), sung three times

The Advent adventures of Fergie the frog:

The beginning of the adventure:

Narrator: One Saturday morning Fergie the Frog and his best friend Roger decided to go exploring. They each packed a lunch of fly-loaf sandwiches and Swamp Soda. 'Be home in time for supper,' called Mother Frog.

Fergie: Sure thing, Mum. We're just going to explore the stream.

Roger: Come on, Fergie. Let's get going.

Narrator: Fergie and Roger set off through the trees towards the stream. They left their packs on a sunny log and played leapfrog on the bank of the stream for most of the morning. Then they practised diving off an old stump into the sparkling water.

As the sun rose towards noon, the two explorers came back to the old log lying on the edge of the stream. The sun had made it warm and dry.

Roger: This is a perfect spot for lunch, Fergie.

Narrator: So Fergie and Roger opened their packs while they sat on the log.

Fergie: Ick, mum put mustard on my fly-loaf. I can't eat mustard.

Narrator: He tossed his sandwich on the grass.

Roger: Here. You can have half my sandwich.

Narrator: After lunch, the two little frogs stretched out on the log to watch the clouds float by. Soon they were dozing in the sunshine as the water gently rocked the log … When Fergie woke up, the log had floated into the middle of the stream.

Fergie: Hey, Roger! This is neat! Let's play Huckleberry Frog floating down the river!

Narrator: The two explorers had a great time that afternoon pretending the log was a raft. Then it became an important ship sailing in the ocean. The sailors were so busy that they didn't notice how swiftly the water was flowing. Suddenly they heard the roar of water not too far away.

Fergie: A waterfall!

Roger: What are we going to do?!

Fergie: Jump! Let's swim for it.

Narrator: But when Roger jumped, the water pulled him towards the waterfall. Fergie stayed on the log, clinging by his toes. Roger swirled along in the water beside the log. They were headed straight for the waterfall …

Worship leader:

What will happen next? We'll have to wait to find out!

Sometimes we find ourselves in the middle of trouble – and we just have to wait to find out how things will work out.

Waiting in the middle of trouble is a hard thing to do – but it happens to everybody sometime.

So when you find yourself in the middle of trouble, it's good to remember God is right beside you, loving you, shining God's love into your trouble to help you find your way.

So turn on your candle light and let's sing our 'trouble song' together …

Song: 'This little light of mine' (sung three times)

The middle of the adventure:

Narrator: Both little frogs went right over the waterfall. The log hit a rock as it came over the falls. The jolt sent Fergie flying through the air. He landed – kerplop! – on the soft moss on the bank. Fergie shook himself to see if he was OK.

Fergie: Roger? Where are you?

Narrator: At first, Fergie couldn't see his friend. Then he heard a little voice.

Roger: … Help …

Narrator: The splash and gurgle of the water swallowed up the sound. Fergie peered over the bank of the stream. Roger was caught in a little whirlpool at the bottom of the waterfall. Every time he got his nose out of the water, he was sucked back in.

Roger: … Help …

Narrator: Roger sputtered again. Then he disappeared into the whirlpool. Fergie looked around for something to rescue Roger. He spotted a silver thread in the grass.

Fergie: Fishing line! Maybe I can rescue Roger.

Narrator: He pulled on the line, which was attached to a plastic fishing floatball caught in some weeds. Fergie tugged the line free and tossed the ball into the water. The whirlpool sucked the ball down into the swirling water. But sure enough, when it bobbed back to the surface, Roger was hanging on to the ball for dear life.

Fergie: *(yelling)* Don't let go, Roger!

Narrator: He began to pull on the fishing line. A few minutes later Roger and the ball were safe on shore. Both little frogs sank into the mud. They were so tired!

Roger: *(groaning)* My legs hurt. Too much frog-paddling! Let's rest for a while before we go home, Fergie.

Fergie: Home? How are we going to get home? We landed on the wrong side of the stream. Home is on the other side.

Roger: Oh no! What are we going to do now?

Narrator: It was getting dark. Those two frightened little frogs just huddled in the mud, scared and tired and hungry. The next morning, they couldn't find much breakfast, just a mouthful of moss.

Fergie: I wish I had that fly-loaf sandwich, mustard and all.

Narrator: Tired and hungry, Fergie and Roger set out to find their way home.

Roger: Let's hop back along this side of the stream, past the waterfall, until the water is calm enough for us to swim across.

Fergie: OK. I wish I were a bird right now. It would be so much faster to fly.

Narrator: They hopped along the bank right beside the water, so they wouldn't get lost. Suddenly Roger cried,

Roger: Look, Fergie! Over there. It's a blue heron!

Fergie: Are you sure? Maybe it's just a sandpiper. Or a very tall seagull.

Roger: Nope, it's a blue heron. And they love little frogs for breakfast. Quick! Hide!

Narrator: Fergie and Roger hopped as fast as fleas into the forest and hid under some toadstools. And that's where we'll find them in the next episode!

Worship leader:

In the middle of trouble, we can get pretty scared. Some days, all we can do is take a deep breath and say a prayer for God to help us through the trouble. So turn on your candle again, and let's sing our trouble song to help us find the courage to keep going.

Song: 'This little light of mine' (three times)

The end of the adventure:

Narrator: The two little frogs sat as still as they could, even though they were shaking. When they figured the heron had finished its breakfast, they set off again, hopping through the woods. Every time they heard a noise, they would dive under some leaves until it was quiet again.

Fergie: What's that?

Narrator: They could see some leaves moving on the ground ahead of them.

Roger: *(whispering)* It could be a snake.

Fergie: What kind of snake? A garter snake?

Roger: No, something bigger. Maybe a bull snake.

Fergie: Or maybe a boa constrictor!

Narrator: Roger frowned.

Roger: There are no boa constrictors here, Fergie. They live in the jungle.

Narrator: But just then the leaves on the ground rustled again.

Fergie: *(yelling)* Hop for the hills! A snake can only eat one of us at a time!

Narrator: So Roger hopped off one way and Fergie headed the other. A few minutes later, Fergie stopped. He was puffing.

Fergie: Roger? Where are you? ... Roger?

Narrator: There was no answer. Fergie hopped a little further, but he stopped when he heard a sound.

Fergie: Roger? Come out. Stop hiding.

Narrator: There was still no answer. Then some leaves rustled behind him. Fergie froze.

Fergie: The snake! It really *is* a boa constrictor, no matter what Roger says!

Narrator: Fergie sat very, very still, hoping the snake in the leaves behind him would fall asleep.

Fergie: And then, when it isn't looking, I'll make a hop for it.

Narrator: In a few minutes he thought it would be safe so he got ready to jump. But as soon as Fergie bent his knees, the leaves rustled behind him. So Fergie sat very still again.

Meanwhile, a search party was on its way. Mother Frog knew something was wrong when Fergie missed supper. 'He never misses bug burgers and french flies,' she said. 'Our explorers must be lost in the woods.'

So early next morning, the Frog family set out to find the explorers. Fergie's brother Freddie found the place where our explorers had eaten lunch the day before. 'Look! This has to be Fergie's leftover sandwich. He won't eat fly-loaf if it has mustard on it,' said Freddie.

'But where can those two be? Their tracks stop here,' said Mother Frog.

'They wouldn't have gone any closer to the waterfall,' said Father Frog. 'No son of mine could be that crazy!'

'Let's swim across the stream and see if they are on the other side,' Freddie suggested. 'It's easy to get lost over there.'

So the Frog family swam the stream in search of clues. They poked in the tall grass and called, 'Fergie! Roger! Where are you?' Suddenly, there was a wild scrambling in the brush. A little voice called,

Roger: Help! Help! Help! The snake, the snake, the snake!

Narrator:	'It's Roger!' cried Freddie. Sure enough, Roger bounced out of the bushes, yelping 'Help!' on every hop!
Roger:	Help! Help! Help! The boa constrictor has eaten Fergie. I can't find him anywhere.
Narrator:	Father Frog said, 'Settle down, Roger. There are no boa constrictors in our forest. What happened to you two?'
	Roger tumbled out the tale of the explorers' adventure. Then Mother Frog and Freddie took him home while Father Frog went to find Fergie. And there was Fergie, sitting perfectly still, deep in the forest.
Fergie:	*(whispering)* Dad … Oh, Dad!
Narrator:	Fergie's lips were tight with fear.
Fergie:	I'm sitting on a snake. Every time I move, it moves. It must be hungry by now. It ate Roger for breakfast.
Narrator:	Father Frog smiled. 'Roger is safe at home by now. And you are sitting perfectly still on a tree branch. When you move, it jiggles and rattles its leaves. There is no snake, Fergie.' Fergie's eyes bulged.
Fergie:	You're kidding.
Narrator:	Ever so slowly he turned his head to see his snake, which wore long antlers of maple leaves *(use whatever tree is common in your area)*. Carefully Fergie peeked underneath himself.
Fergie:	Argh! I've been sitting here on a stupid branch of maple leaves all morning, waiting for it to eat me.
Narrator:	Father Frog chuckled. 'Yup! You're a pretty brave explorer, wrestling that stick to the ground! Let's go home. You must be hungry.'
Fergie:	Right! Do you think I could have breakfast, lunch and supper all together?

Narrator: His father smiled and nodded. 'With no mustard.'

Worship leader:

Now sometimes we have to wait quite a while to get through some trouble. God's people have to learn to wait with God to get through our troubles and find our way.

The Sundays in December are Sundays when we practise waiting with God in the middle of the troubles in the world. As we light one candle at a time, we remember that God's people waited a long time for Jesus to bring his light into the world. Sometimes God's people were afraid while they waited. Sometimes they didn't know what would happen next. But still they waited and hoped for God to shine more light into the world.

Finally Jesus came to shine God's light into the world more brightly. Jesus still brings God's light into any trouble we face to show us the way through. So as we wait for Christmas to come, let's give thanks that God is always with us when we're waiting. And God's light will always shine for us in Jesus!

Now let's sing another song about how we can shine God's light for each other. You can turn on your candles again!

Song: 'Jesus bids us shine' (various songbooks)

Offering

Prayers of God's children:

These prayers were written by Grade 3 schoolchildren, who used Fergie's stories in class and then wrote their own prayer book.

Voice one: Dear God, thank you for all your creations – animals, plants, trees and water; rain, food and sunshine. Thank you for my life and the world I live in.

Leader: Hear the voice of your children praying, O God.
All: Make us light for the world you love.

Voice two: Thank you, God, for this day. During this night, please make sure that the night is safe, not just for me but for everybody.
Leader: Hear the voice of your children praying, O God.
All: Make us light for the world you love.

Voice one: Dear Lord, thank you for our families, moms, dads, brothers, sisters. Although we fight and have arguments, I love them. The memories, the times, the laughter, the pleasure I will always remember. Thank you for my family.
Leader: Hear the voice of your children praying, O God.
All: Make us light for the world you love.

Voice two: Dear God, give us your love when we are upset. Help us to tell someone we are angry and lonely. And please help us to be good.
Leader: Hear the voice of your children praying, O God.
All: Make us light for the world you love.

Voice one: O Lord, help the sick get well. For those who feel ill, keep them safe.
Leader: Hear the voice of your children praying, O God.
All: Make us light for the world you love.

Voice two: Dear God, please help the homeless and the poor. Give them strength to go on with their lives without sorrow. And bring laughter to all of the children who are poor.
Leader: Hear the voice of your children praying, O God.
All: Make us light for the world you love.

Leader: God, we pray to you from the lips of all your children in every situation we face, young or old, big or small. Make us light for the world you love, in Jesus' name. Amen

Song: 'I am the light of the world', by Jim Strathdee, Desert Flower Music; or 'Christ, be our light', by Bernadette Farrell, CH4 543

Bible reading: (Matthew 5:14–16)

Voice one: Jesus said: You are the light of the world.

Voice two: No one after lighting a lamp puts it under the bushel basket, but on the lampstand, and it gives light to all in the house.

Voice one: In the same way, let your light shine before others, so that they may see your good works and give glory to your Father in heaven.

All: Jesus, we will let our little lights shine in the world in your name.

Blessing

What are you waiting for?
A service for Advent

Dave Broom

Folk gather around a central table, which is covered in clocks with tea-lights (unlit and enough for the whole congregation) randomly placed between them. Keep the first part of the service fairly dark to provide a contrast with later on, when the candles are lit.

The lighting of the Advent candle

Opening responses

God of time and God of eternity
FOR YOU WE WAIT.

God of outer space and God closer than we can imagine
FOR YOU WE WAIT.

God of the roaring noise of the world and God of silence
FOR YOU WE WAIT.

In our homes, classrooms, factories, offices and fields
FOR YOU WE WAIT.

In this place and in this time
FOR YOU WE WAIT.

Song or hymn: 'O come, O come Emmanuel' (CH4 273)

Prayer

God of Advent, of darkness, of waiting,
we wait ...
for the hungry to be fed,
for freedom for all,
for the weapons of war to be abolished,
for everyone to have clean water and sanitation,
for an end to suspicion between Christian, Muslim and Jew,
for peace in our world ...

God of Advent, of darkness, of waiting,
we wait ...
for your Kingdom to come.

Bible reading: Revelation 22:1–17 (The Coming of Jesus, Good News Bible)

Reflection

Time: the mathematical measurement of our days, our weeks, our years.

We use many words to talk about time: A generation stands between us and the people born 20 or 30 years later or earlier. A decade is often the way we review political and social change, take 'the roaring twenties' or 'the swinging sixties', for example. There are great periods of time: antiquity, the Dark Ages, the Renaissance, the Enlightenment, the Victorian era, and so on.

An hour, a week, a fortnight, a decade, a millennium ... All of these periods help us to mark and quantify time, to say when something started and when it ended.

We also talk about time in other ways: 'I'll see you soon', 'I won't be long', 'I go there now and again', 'I've been waiting for ages' ...

These phrases are not precise. This is time experienced not time quantified. Time can drag and time can fly. We can feel we never have *enough* time, or that we have too much time on our hands ... If it's nearly the end of the match and our football team is one goal up, time seems to slow down unbelievably. If we're at a great party with good friends – time seems to go by in a flash.

We might wait for hours for a special person with whom we have a date, but we probably wouldn't wait that long for a bus to the next town!

This is our time of waiting ...

What are you waiting for?

What are you waiting for?

Voice 1:   I'm waiting to see if my lottery numbers come up. I'm sure I'll win this week!

Voice 2:   I'm waiting for my boyfriend – he's always late!

Voice 3:   I'm waiting to see the new James Bond film – Daniel Craig is definitely the best Bond!

Voice 4:   I'm waiting for the pub to open.

Voice 5:   I'm waiting for the bathroom – how much longer?!

Voice 6:   I'm waiting for my car to be fixed … and I've been waiting *all day*. What are they doing?!

Voice 7:   I'm waiting for a lift. Hitchhiking is no good if you want to get somewhere fast!

Voice 8:   I'm waiting for things to get better.

All voices: Waiting, waiting, waiting …

The waiting room

(Go straight into this script following the 8 voices.)

Questioner: Evening.

Waiting person: Evening.

Questioner: You been here long?

Waiting person: Not that long, about … 2,000 years, I suppose, give or take …

Questioner: What!

Waiting person: Well, he said he was coming soon, so I've just been hanging around, I suppose, waiting …

Questioner: For 2,000 years!

Waiting person: Well, when you say it like that I admit it does seem like a long time, but it's gone by quite fast.

Questioner: Quite fast! Quite fast! Whole civilisations have risen and fallen in that time. World wars have been fought. Tyrants and kings have plundered and persecuted. Great advances in science and technology have been made. Terrible atrocities have been wrought. The atom bomb was invented for crying out loud, and you say you've just been 'hanging around'!

Waiting person: All right, all right, don't get in a tizzy. All I know is: he said he was coming soon, and I've been sitting here waiting for him to arrive. Look, I've got a cup of tea here ready for him, just the way he likes it.

Questioner: Be a bit cold now.

Waiting person: What?!

Questioner: Er, nothing, nothing, I just said, haven't you been cold?

Waiting person: Well, it's been a bit chilly at times, I admit. Napoleon's retreat from Moscow was a bit draughty, and the siege of Stalingrad – my word that was a cold one! But there have been happier times: the coronation of Queen Victoria, now that was nice, and that Martin Luther King, he was a lovely man, and I did enjoy listening to the Beatles.

Questioner: But haven't you ever given up hope? Don't you think he might not come back at all now? I mean, it's been a very long time, hasn't it?

Waiting person: Oh, no, he said he'd be back, and when he does I'll be here waiting for him!

Questioner: You do know that theologians now think that he won't be back, well not in quite the same way … not in the way you're thinking anyhow. They call it 'Realised Eschatology' these days …

Waiting person: Realised what?!

Questioner: Eschatology: the study of the end times. We've kind of left all that Hieronymus Bosch Final Judgement, ash clouds and sulphur stuff behind.

Waiting person: Really?! I'd heard it was still pretty popular in some places: the Rapture, the last days, prophets and prophecies. That Ronald Reagan, he was pretty interested in it by all accounts.

Questioner: Yes – and since his finger was on the nuclear trigger he was liable to cause it!

You see, the early Christians, as you'll know, they thought that Jesus was about to come back at any minute, but they were facing horrible persecution under Nero or Domitian. You can't blame them for hoping they'd be rescued. But now we tend to think that all those odd passages in the New Testament refer to Jesus' ministry: to the Kingdom of God being here, now, among us. It's not the end of the world we should be looking for, but rather its rebirth, instituted by Jesus.

Waiting person: Really?! But Jesus said he was definitely coming back. It's all here in scripture: a triumphal return, clouds, lightning from east to west and all the rest of it. Why do you think I've been sitting here? I don't think much of your realised esk-a-whatnot – sounds like a bit of a cop-out to me!

Questioner: But why would God want to destroy the world? That's so life-denying. This is a beautiful world. It's pretty messed up in places, granted, but God wants us to be his ambassadors, his activists and to work and struggle for peace and justice in *this* world.

Waiting person: Well, I *have* wondered about that while I've been sitting here. I've often wanted to ask God what he was doing about hunger and poverty, about corruption and the arms trade and all the rest of it.

Questioner: Well, why don't you? Why don't you ask God what he's doing?

Waiting person: ... Because I'm frightened he might ask me the same question.

Introduction to the symbolic action

What are you waiting for? In this season of the Church's year we wait, not for turkey and tinsel, mass consumerism and waste, but in expectation, in hope – for a God who comes to us as a refugee born in an obscure village in Roman-occupied Palestine.

We wait for God, but God also waits for us. 'Go into all the world,' Jesus tells us, 'and make disciples of all nations.' The call to discipleship is about putting the demands of God's Kingdom first. We ask God that the poor may find food, that the homeless may find shelter, that war may be abolished, that the pollution of the environment may end, and God asks us: 'Well, what are you going to do about it? How are you, my disciples, going to make a difference?' ...

Tonight we sang the beautiful hymn 'O come, O come Emmanuel': Emmanuel: God-with-us, God who identifies with, and becomes part of, the human condition. God who empowers us to dream of a new world of justice and peace.

What will this Advent mean to you? What will you do differently as a result of the past year? How will you commit yourself to the demands of the Kingdom to bring Good News to the poor, liberty to the captives, recovery of sight to the blind and freedom to the oppressed?

Spend a little time now thinking about what you can do. Is there a cause you want to become more involved in? Is there something you started doing that maybe you've let drop a bit in recent years or months and want to pick up again? Is there something you know you could be good at? ...

Time of reflection ...

At the beginning of the service we lit a candle, a traditional practice during Advent. On the table are clocks surrounded by candles. During the singing of the next chant ('Wait for the Lord', Taizé, CH4 276 or 'Come light, light of God', CH4 784) I invite you to come and light one of the candles: as a symbol of your commitment to become more practically involved in God's world.

'You know what time it is,' Paul writes to the church in Rome. *'Now is the moment for you to wake from sleep. For salvation is nearer to us now than when we became believers; the night is far gone, the day is near. Let us then lay aside the works of darkness and put on the armour of light.'* (Romans 13:11–12, NRSV)

Come, Emmanuel, God-with-us, and make us a people who bring about change in your world – and who help your Kingdom come.

Symbolic action *(lighting candles)*

Prayer

God of Advent,
among refugees and outcasts
you breathed your first breaths.
In the cry of a newborn child you proclaimed
Emmanuel, God-with-us.
Come, God of the margins,
breathe into us the spirit of longing for your Kingdom.
Come this Advent to make us dream of
and work for
a better world of justice and freedom.
Come, Lord, come.
Amen

Blessing

*'I, Jesus, have sent my angel to announce these things to you in the churches.
I am descended from the family of David; I am the bright morning star.'*

The Spirit and the Bride say, 'Come!'
Everyone who hears this must also say, 'Come!'

Come, whoever is thirsty; accept the water of life as a gift, whoever wants it.

(Revelation 22:16–17, Good News Bible)

May the God of Advent,
the God of waiting,
the God with us,
bless us all now and evermore.
Amen

Waiting in darkness

An Advent liturgy

David McNeish & Sarah Anderson

This evening liturgy is most effective in a setting in which it is possible to sit for a while in darkness. If this is not possible, then the lower the lighting the better.

Three large candles are lit before the service begins. A tea-light is given to each person as they arrive. All the lights are on as folk take their seats.

A bell is rung to start the service; this can be a handbell.

(Lights begin to be turned off.)

Solo singing voice (slowly, at about half-speed):

First verse of 'Longing for light, we wait in darkness', by Bernadette Farrell (CH4 543)

(More lights are turned off.)

Spoken voice:

The darkness at this time of year can be overwhelming.
And it only increases our craving for light.

(More lights are turned off.)

Longing can sap our strength.
Until turning towards truth becomes
the most difficult of tasks.

(More lights are turned off, until only the candles are left lit.)

All too often, the light we long for is delayed ...

(The candles are blown out.)

And we are left to contemplate the darkness.

We are still together, but we are also alone.
We are still hopeful, but we are also unsure.
We are still. Still in darkness ...

As we sit in silence, reflect on how you feel about the dark: on what emotions and memories it evokes.

We take some time now to do this ...

(The length of time to leave for the silence depends on how familiar people are with silent contemplation. Anything from 2 minutes to 20 may be appropriate.)

Solo singing voice:

Second verse of 'Longing for light, we wait in darkness'

Spoken voice:

We do not choose the darkness,
and few are comfortable within it.
In the absence of light
our hearts whisper their secrets,
and loss and pain
seep from the corners
to disquiet our minds.

And yet,
all life begins in darkness.
In the womb, the cocoon,
life grows,
and waits,
and gathers strength.
For those who find the courage to dwell there
the darkness can hold treasure
and truth.

And so we wait,
listening to the stories of our hearts,
knowing that we are held safe
in a deeper story of Love,
in which the Light
will always return.

(Pause)

(The three candles are re-lit. This is particularly effective if the sound of the striking match can be captured by a microphone.)

The prophet Isaiah speaks of the servant of light:

Here is my servant, whom I uphold,
my chosen, in whom my soul delights;
I have put my spirit upon him;
he will bring forth justice to the nations.
He will not cry or lift up his voice,
or make it heard in the street;
a bruised reed he will not break,
and a dimly burning wick he will not quench;
he will faithfully bring forth justice.
He will not grow faint or be crushed
until he has established justice in the earth;
and the coastlands wait for his teaching.

(Isaiah 42:1–4, NRSV)

Our longing can feel inadequate.
IT IS NOT.

Our cries may feel insignificant.
THEY ARE NOT.

We may so easily grow faint.
CHRIST WILL NOT.

Our strength may be weak, our light may be dim,
BUT A BRUISED REED HE WILL NOT BREAK,
AND A DIMLY BURNING WICK HE WILL NOT QUENCH.

The light flickers, but it will endure:
UNTIL HE HAS ESTABLISHED JUSTICE ON THE EARTH.

So come,
add your wick
to the light of the world.

ALL WHO LONG FOR JUSTICE:
add your wick
to the light of the world.

ALL WHO CRAVE ACCEPTANCE:
add your wick
to the light of the world.

ALL WHO ENDURE HATRED:
add your wick
to the light of the world.

ALL WHO FEEL THEY HAVE LITTLE TO OFFER:
add your wick
to the light of the world.

ALONE WE FALTER, TOGETHER WE BLAZE.
We follow the light we have,
AND PRAY FOR MORE LIGHT.

You are invited to come and light your candle from one of the three central candles, and as you do, to remember a situation in your community or in the world that is in need of more light.

This time of prayer can be silent, or people can be encouraged to mention situations out loud, with the congregation responding. For example:

In the West Bank and Gaza:
LET LIGHT SHINE.

In our family's illness:
LET LIGHT SHINE.

Hymn: 'Longing for light, we wait in darkness' (CH4 543)

Blessing:

It is dark outside.
But we carry into the night
the light of Christ.
MAY THE LIGHT OF CHRIST SHINE IN OUR MIDST,
KEEPING AWAY ALL THAT WOULD SEEK TO HARM,
ESTABLISHING ALL THAT GOD'S LOVE DEMANDS,
THIS NIGHT AND ALWAYS.
AMEN

Bread of life
An all-age Communion for Lent

Nancy Cocks

Leader:

God calls us to worship. Jesus said, 'I am the bread of life. Whoever comes to me will never be hungry. Whoever believes in me will never be thirsty.'

Song: 'Lord, listen to your children praying', by Ken Medema, Hope Publishing (sing through three or four times)

A prayer to offer God our love:

God, we are so glad to be part of your family – young and old, big and small, women and men, boys and girls. You reach out in love to each one of us. You call us by our names because you know us through and through. Help us remember to put your family first in all we do so that everyone who sees us will know that we are Jesus' friends and followers who love you with all our hearts. Amen

Our prayer to say sorry to God (said together):

God, you came to share our life in Jesus, to show us how to share our lives with others. We're sorry we don't always share what we have. We like to keep our own things to ourselves. Even in our families it's not easy to share with each other. Forgive us when we hang on to our own stuff too tightly. Open our hearts and our hands to share what we have, in Jesus' name. Amen

We hear a kind word from God:

Friends, remember what Saint Paul said. He asked if anything could separate us from God's love that we meet in Jesus. Hardship? Trouble? Things going wrong?

'No,' he said, 'we can always stay standing through God's love.'

So remember: whenever things go wrong, Jesus offers you a hand to get you back on your feet!

And so God's people said:

All: Amen!

A word about bread:

Conversation led by the worship leader

- How many people ate bread this morning? Toast? Did everyone eat their crusts?

- Bread is one of the most common foods all over the world.

- 5000 years ago people were eating bread in Egypt.

- Eating bread changed the way people lived: people began to grow grain instead of hunting and chasing animals all over the place.

- There are many different kinds of bread, made out of different kinds of grain.

- What kinds of bread do you eat at your house?

- White bread, whole wheat, rye bread? Crackers? Cornbread?

- Gluten-free bread?

- Muffins, pancakes, biscuits, waffles, buns, fried bread, bannock?

- Banana bread, fruit bread – cake?

- Pita bread, pizza, naan bread, mantou bread from China?

- Bread is so important to people everywhere that sometimes we say 'bread' when we really mean all the food we need every day.

- Jesus taught us to pray for our 'daily bread' – that prayer reminds us we trust God to give us all the food we need to live healthy lives in God's world.

Listen to the story Jesus told about our daily bread:

Bible readings:

(Use one or several different voices)

Reading: Luke 11:1–5:

> One of Jesus' disciples said to him, 'Lord, teach us to pray.' And Jesus said, 'When you pray, say: Our Father in heaven, hallowed be your name. Your kingdom come. Give us each day our daily bread. And forgive us our sins, for we ourselves forgive everyone who owes us something. And do not bring us to the time of trial.'

Sung response: 'Lord, listen to your children praying'

Reading: Luke 11:5–8:

> Later Jesus said to his friends, 'Suppose one of you has a friend, and you go to him at midnight and say to him, "Friend, lend me three loaves of bread, for another friend of mine has just arrived, and I have nothing to feed him." But what if that first friend answered, "Don't bother me! Our door is already locked for the night. My children and I are in bed. I can't get up and give you anything." What would you do then? I tell you, if you really needed bread, you'd keep knocking. And your friend would get up and get the bread because you kept asking.'

Sung response

Reading: Luke 11:9–10:

> So Jesus said, 'Ask, and it will be given to you; search, and you will find; knock, and the door will be opened for you. For everyone who asks receives, and everyone who searches finds, and for everyone who knocks, the door will be opened.'

Sung response

Breaking bread, a drama:

(Features parts for 3 voices and a narrator)

Voice one: Look, Mama! My bread! It's done. It's perfect!

Narrator: Hannah smiled as she pulled her very first loaf of bread from the oven. Hannah's mother nodded. 'Why don't you take it to your grandmother, dear? She will be very pleased. She could eat your fine bread for the Sabbath tomorrow.' So Hannah set out for her grandmother's, carrying her precious loaf of bread in a basket. Her brother Joel called:

Voice two: Give me a taste, Hannah! See if I survive your baking!

Voice one: Not from this loaf, Joel. This one is for grandmother. Wait until next week. I'll bake one for you – with a stone in it!

Narrator: Hannah skipped through the streets of Jerusalem. Soon she came upon a blind beggar sitting in a doorway. He cried out:

Voice two: Alms, alms!

Voice one: I have no money.

Voice two: Then a crust of that bread I can smell. Just enough for the Sabbath.

Voice one: I'm sorry. This bread is for my grandmother's Sabbath. But I will bring you bread next week.

Voice two: Bless you, little girl! Next week!

Narrator: The beggar smiled as Hannah hurried on her way. As she turned a corner, she stopped. A crowd pushed down the road. Soldiers shoved people this way and that. Three prisoners dragged the heavy beams for their crosses through the dust. 'Stand back!' the soldiers ordered. Hannah squeezed between two houses.

Voice one: Oh dear, those men will die before the Sabbath. Go with God, I pray.

Narrator: Just then she felt a wet nose on her hand. A street dog licked her fingers.

Voice one: No! I know you are hungry but this bread is for grandmother. I will look for you next week.

Narrator: Around the corner two children caught up with Hannah. Jesse asked:

Voice two: What are you doing, Hannah? Will you play with us?

Narrator: His little sister Rachel piped up:

Voice three: We are going to pick some oranges for breakfast.

Voice one: I'm sorry, I have to take this bread to my grandmother. Haven't you had breakfast yet?

Narrator: Jesse frowned.

Voice two: Since mother died, we have to find our own breakfast.

Voice one: Next week I will bake bread for your breakfast! But I must get to grandmother's now.

Narrator: Just as Hannah reached her grandmother's, it seemed like the earth trembled.

Voice one: Grandmother, are you all right? I brought you some bread.

Narrator: Her grandmother rose from her bed.

Voice three: Here I am, Hannah. Now what have you brought me?

Narrator: Hannah held up her basket.

Voice one: This is the first loaf of bread I ever baked, Grandmother. I brought it for your Sabbath meal.

Voice three: How round and smooth it is. You will be a fine baker when you have grown, Hannah.

Narrator: Her grandmother took the loaf and tore off a piece. Hannah gulped. Her fine round loaf was in two pieces.

Voice one: Grandmother, don't you like it?

Voice three: I could never eat a whole loaf by myself, my dear. But I will wrap up this piece for my Sabbath. You take the rest home.

Narrator: Suddenly the sky went dark.

Voice one: Grandmother, what's wrong?

Voice three: I've never seen anything like this in all my years. First, the whole earth shakes. Now the sky is black. Hannah, we must pray to God to keep us.

Narrator: Together Hannah and her grandmother knelt and prayed:

Voices one
and three: Our Father in heaven, holy is your name. Your kingdom come. Give us each day our daily bread; and forgive us our sins, as we forgive everyone who sins against us; save us from the time of trial.

Narrator: Hannah whispered:

Voice one: Grandmother, this is the Rabbi's prayer.

Voice three: Yes, dear. What we have learned from Jesus, our teacher, we must remember every day. Now you must go. Go with God, little one.

Narrator: As Hannah carried the rest of her loaf homeward, she remembered the words of the prayer, 'Give us each day our daily bread.' She looked around for Rachel and Jesse. They stood at a corner, peeling a single orange.

Voice one: Here, take a piece of my bread for your breakfast.

Narrator: Then Hannah ran off. She had to search for the blind beggar hidden in his doorway.

Voice one: Here, have a piece of my loaf for your Sabbath.

Voice two: Bless you, my child.

Narrator: He stuffed a bit of bread in his mouth as Hannah turned. As she reached the gate of her yard, Hannah saw Joel running, with a street dog at his heels. She smiled:

Voice one: Hey, you two dogs! Let's share the rest of this loaf.

Narrator: They sat under a tree and Hannah tore the bread into chunks. The dog wagged its tail and Joel nodded:

Voice two: Tastes pretty good for a first loaf.

Voice one: Just wait until next week! There will be more bread where this came from. Just like Jesus prayed.

Song (a simple musical setting of the Lord's Prayer)

The Offering

A child-friendly service of communion:

(If communion is not served, go on to the Prayers of the people.)

Invitation to communion:

Come and see the gifts of God's love,
laid on this table waiting for you.
Come and touch the gifts of God's love for you,
love as fresh as sliced baked bread,
love as lively as wine on the tongue.
Come and taste the goodness of God,
broken open and poured out for you in Jesus' life and death.
Come and share the goodness of God, in Jesus' name.
Wherever you've come from, whatever your age,
come and know that all this is for you.
Whoever you are, wherever you've been, whatever you've done,
all this is for you when you receive these gifts
with all your heart, strength, mind and soul.

Communion song: 'Let us break bread together' (African American Spiritual, various songbooks)

(The bread and wine are brought forward to the table during the song.)

Celebrant: Listen! Learn why we share bread and wine today. Our meal of bread and wine was started long ago. Each time we gather we remember what it means to us. At important Jewish meals, a young person asks questions about what the family is going to do. Today, one of our children will ask questions about the family meal we share in Jesus' name:

The story of the table:

Child: What are we going to do at this table?

Celebrant: First, we will say a prayer to thank God for everything God has given us. Then, we will break a loaf of bread in pieces and pass the pieces around the whole church so everyone who wants to can have a taste. We will pass these cups of wine *(juice for young people)* around the whole church, too, so everyone who wants to can have a sip.

Child: Why do we share bread and wine?

Celebrant: We share bread and wine today because Jesus shared bread and wine with his friends long ago. It was the same night when Jesus was arrested, on the night before he died. That night he asked his friends to keep sharing bread and wine to remember him.

Child: But I wasn't there with Jesus. What should I remember?

Celebrant: When you take a bit of bread, you should remember that Jesus lived a life like yours. He shared bread with his friends and with everyone who needed it.

When you sip the wine or juice, you should remember that Jesus died because he loves you. He died to promise you that God's love is so powerful, there is nothing to be afraid of, not even dying. So when we take this bread and this wine or juice, we remember that Jesus is still with us.

Just as the bread we eat fills our bodies and the wine we drink warms our hearts, Jesus fills us and warms us with his love every day, every place we go.

So now we are going to do as Jesus did. Just as Jesus gave God thanks for the gifts of the earth, we will thank God for everything too.

The great prayer of thanksgiving:

(Announce any sung responses used in this prayer so children know what to expect, which words to use.)

Celebrant: God who makes us wonder, Maker of all that is:
we bless you for every good gift in the world –
for snow and sunshine to make it sparkle,
for starlight in the deep night sky,
for seeds waking up as the spring comes closer.
We bless you for the food we eat and water to drink,
gifts of this good old earth.
We join our voices with all these amazing things
to praise you for the life you give us.

Chant: 'Santo, santo, santo', CH4 769 (or some other Sanctus easy for children to sing)

Jesus, you walk beside us day by day.
It is so good to know that you lived a life like ours,
walked in the sun, got tired, had sore feet.
It's even better to know you enjoyed your food
and sitting down with your good friends for a meal.
You laughed and you cried.
And you played with children in the town square.
We thank you that you lived on earth and died on earth

to show us how to find God
in the middle of everything that happens.
Here and now you meet us and feed us at this table,
just as all your other friends around the world
meet you at theirs.[1]

Chant

Holy Spirit, Breath of God, breathe on us now
and on these gifts of bread and wine.
As we taste the bread, make us remember
that God will always give us everything we need to live.
As we sip our cups,
make us remember that you are God's love within us
to show how to share everything we have
with neighbours in need
and make the world a wonderful place to live in.
As often as we eat bread or drink wine in Jesus' name
help us remember that your love will never let us go.
Amen

Celebrant: *(breaking the bread)* Jesus said, 'I am the Bread of Life. Take this to remember me.'

(lifting the cup) Jesus said, 'I am the vine and you are my branches.' This is the cup of joy. Drink from it, all of you, to remember Jesus.

These are the gifts of God for the people of God.
Taste and see that God is good.

After everyone has received bread and wine:

Celebrant: The peace of our Lord Jesus Christ be with you.

All: And also with you!

Prayers of the people:

Time of open prayer for those in the world/community who are hungry and who struggle for their daily bread ...

A prayer for God to go with us:

Loving God, your love is as close to us as our own hands and feet.
People who need your love are as close to us
as the people beside us, behind us and in front of us.
Send us now into your world to love each other,
sure that you love us.
Show us where we are needed and how we can make a difference
so that the world will be a good place for all your people.
We know this is what Jesus wanted.
Help us live for Jesus wherever we go.
Amen

Closing song: (something easy and fun for the children to sing)

Closing responses

Blessing

Source:

1. Second stanza of the 'Great prayer of thanksgiving' taken/adapted from a prayer by Kathy Galloway in *The Pattern of Our Days: Liturgies and Resources for Worship*, Kathy Galloway, Wild Goose Publications

A liturgy for
the Feast of the Transfiguration
Hiroshima Day, 6th August

Norman Shanks

Opening responses:

Ever-present God, around us, within us,
WE COME TO PRAISE AND WORSHIP YOU.

God of eternity, God of the here and now,
WE COME SEEKING TO SERVE YOU.

God of the big picture, whose loving purpose embraces the whole world,
WE COME TO STRENGTHEN OUR COMMITMENT.

God of the smallest detail, closer to us than breathing,
WE COME TO INCREASE OUR DISCERNMENT.

God of the rhinoceros and the midge,
God of the Large Hadron Collider and the iPhone,
HELP US TO SENSE YOUR PRESENCE IN AND THROUGH ALL THINGS.

God whose grace is sufficient for all our needs,
HELP US TO BE PEOPLE OF COMPASSION, JUSTICE AND PEACE.

Bible readings: St Luke 9:28–36, 2 Corinthians 5:16–6:2

Reflection:

Over 50 years ago, in December 1965, in the Iona Community's magazine, *Coracle*, George MacLeod, the Community's founder and leader at the time, wrote a characteristically powerful article focussing on the dropping of the atomic bomb on Hiroshima on 6 August 1945, the date widely celebrated by Churches all over the world as the Feast of the Transfiguration. Rooted in his conviction about the fundamental significance of 'matter', he spoke with telling and challengingly imaginative insight of the fusion of the material and the spiritual and affirmed that each atom is permeated, indeed identified with *'the emergent body of Christ'*. Thus, he said, in the Hiroshima bombing: *'we took His body and we took His blood and we enacted a cosmic Golgotha. We took the key to love and we used it for bloody hell.'*[1]

This is a kind of 'reverse transfiguration', almost turning upside down the biblical account of the experience of Peter, James and John in encountering God's glory revealed in the transfigured Jesus on the mountaintop. But it forces us to encounter the stark, down-to-earth reality of nuclear weapons in the here and now. The story of the Transfiguration may seem mysterious and rather abstract, even nebulous – shot through with a wonderful, shining power. But we are reminded that the Hiroshima bomb was perceived as being *'brighter than a thousand suns'* and, as George MacLeod said in 1965, *'that the world potential for perpetrating bloody hell (as "the lesser of two evils") is now a million times Hiroshima'.*

At the heart of Iona Abbey, in the centre of the cloisters, stands a striking statue – *the Descent of the Spirit*, by the Jewish-American sculptor Jacques Lipchitz. Its bomb-like appearance frequently provokes comment and discussion, and it has been the focus of many a reflection – not least on Hiroshima Day – on the urgent imperative of peacemaking in our times. The Feast of the Transfiguration celebrates the promise of new life, the hope that, within the miracle and mystery of God's transforming grace, beyond our banal everyday existence, things can be different; and God's purpose of shalom leaves no place for nuclear weapons. For over 30 years now mainstream churches have spoken out and campaigned against them as inherently evil and morally wrong. Majority public opinion is consistently opposed, and many military voices have called in question the strategic case for their continued possession for such first-strike missiles. Moreover the opportunity costs are massive in a situation of economic 'austerity' and with the urgent need for more spending on services like health, education, social welfare and transport. Arguments about nuclear deterrence 'keeping the peace' and maintaining 'security' are shown to be shallow and illusory in the face of reflection on the true nature of peace and security. The apparent commitment to multilateral disarmament is thin in view of the lack of significant progress and the absence of any moral justification for a stance that refuses to allow other nations to develop a nuclear capacity. In reality the replacement of Trident seemed to have more to do with keeping the UK's seat 'at the top table' within the UN Security Council in a feeble attempt to hold on to international dominance and hark back to an imperial past.

We are called to be *'ambassadors of Christ'* and to share in God's *'ministry of reconciliation'*, guided by the vision and values of God's kingdom. For many of us nuclear disarmament has become virtually a 'confessional issue', an imperative of our Christian commitment, influencing which political party we support, impelling us as a matter of urgency to share in demonstrations, vigils and acts of witness at Faslane (where the Trident submarines are based, only 20 or so miles from Glasgow). The Feast of the Transfiguration strengthens our resolve and encourages our hope: truly 'another world is possible'!

Affirmation of faith:

WE BELIEVE THAT GOD IS PRESENT
IN THE DARKNESS BEFORE DAWN;
IN THE WAITING AND UNCERTAINTY
WHERE FEAR AND COURAGE JOIN HANDS,
CONFLICT AND CARING LINK ARMS,
AND THE SUN RISES OVER BARBED WIRE.

WE BELIEVE IN A WITH-US GOD
WHO SITS DOWN IN OUR MIDST
TO SHARE OUR HUMANITY.

WE AFFIRM A FAITH
THAT TAKES US BEYOND THE SAFE PLACE:
INTO ACTION, INTO VULNERABILITY
AND INTO THE STREETS.

WE COMMIT OURSELVES TO WORK FOR CHANGE
AND PUT OURSELVES ON THE LINE;
TO BEAR RESPONSIBILITY, TAKE RISKS,
LIVE POWERFULLY AND FACE HUMILIATION;
TO STAND WITH THOSE ON THE EDGE;
TO CHOOSE LIFE
AND BE USED BY THE SPIRIT
FOR GOD'S NEW COMMUNITY OF HOPE.
AMEN[2]

Prayer:

Living God,
whose very being is energy and light and love,
too often our lives may seem paralysed into inertia,
overwhelmed by darkness,
bedevilled by hardness of heart.
And we are complicit in the corporate sins of society,
the failures of governments and political leaders
to eradicate injustice and violence
and bring about the international harmony,
the freedom from fear and want that is your purpose
for each and every one of us.

So we seek forgiveness and we pray for grace –
that your transfiguring power may touch our lives,
may strengthen all those who strive for justice and seek to make peace,
that weapons of war may be transformed into instruments of creativity.
We ask this in Jesus' name.
Amen

Closing words:

IN DAYS TO COME MAY OUR LIVES BEAR WITNESS
THAT GOODNESS IS STRONGER THAN EVIL,
LIFE IS STRONGER THAN DEATH.

AS GOD REQUIRES OF US,
MAY WE DO JUSTICE,
LOVE KINDNESS
AND PRACTISE HUMILITY.

THROUGH THE UPS AND DOWNS OF OUR LIVES,
ON THE MOUNTAINTOP, IN THE DEPTHS, DAY BY DAY,
MAY GOD'S SPIRIT HELP US TO STAND FIRM
AND WALK IN GOD'S WAY
AMEN

Sources:

1. From *Coracle*, December 1965. For the complete passage see 'Cosmic Golgotha', *Daily Readings with George MacLeod*, Ron Ferguson (Ed.), Wild Goose Publications, republished 2004

2. From *Iona Abbey Worship Book*, Wild Goose Publications, 2001. This affirmation was composed by two Iona Community members following a protest at Faslane.

A lament for Jesus
& for the crucified of our time
A liturgy for the evening of Good Friday

Chris Polhill

You will need:

- *Two or three trestles used to support a coffin, or a low oblong table or a bench*

- *A full-sized wooden cross*

- *A length of black cloth*

- *A similar length of purple material*

- *Two tall candles*

- *Two or three black buckets (such as those used for gardening or DIY)*

- *Sufficient autumn leaves to fill the buckets*

Setting and opening

Before the service, make space in the church as you would for a coffin. Place the trestles, table or bench in this space and cover over with the black cloth. Set two tall lighted candles at what would be the head of the coffin. Depending on the building, either have the seating around the coffin space, leaving clear room at the head and foot, or have the coffin space at the front of the pews.

All leaders of the service are dressed in black.

Folk gather, sitting quietly …

One leader walks in slowly, and welcomes everyone, making any necessary announcements, and making it clear that the service has no fixed ending and that people should leave in their own time.

Leader: At this service we join the disciples as they come together to bury their friend Jesus. We remember his life, and lament his death. You are invited to stand …

Six or eight people, dressed in black, carry in the cross (in the manner they would a coffin, carrying its weight upon their shoulders; linking inside arms helps stability). They walk with slow reverence to the coffin space as solemn music is played (e.g. 'La Sonodora' by Enya from In Memory of the Trees*). It is well worth practising this, as walking slowly together and placing the cross needs to be well done.*

In time with each other, they lower the cross onto the covered trestles, bench or
table. In time with each other, they turn in to the cross and bow reverently, and
then walk slowly to seats reserved for them. Other leaders of the service follow
the cross in, bow in reverence, and move to their places.

(Divide up the readings in this service between the different leaders.)

Opening prayer (Psalm 22:1–8, NRSV)

My God, my God, why have you forsaken me?
Why are you so far from helping me, from the words of my groaning?
O my God, I cry by day, but you do not answer;
and by night, but find no rest.

Yet you are holy, enthroned on the praises of Israel.
In you our ancestors trusted;
they trusted, and you delivered them.
To you they cried, and were saved;
in you they trusted, and were not put to shame.

But I am a worm, and not human;
scorned by others, and despised by the people.
All who see me mock at me;
they make mouths at me, they shake their heads:
'Commit your cause to the Lord; let him deliver –
let him rescue the one in whom he delights!'

Song: 'Contemplate Christ's sacrifice'; tune: 'Proper Sarum' melody mode/
'Before the ending of the day' (8888)

(Sung unaccompanied, or with a flute playing the melody)

Before your passion, Jesus Christ,
we contemplate your sacrifice;
that staying true to God's own way,
you give your all, true love display.

While leaders played their power game,
your silence put them all to shame.

You taught of costly peace and love,
then showed us on the cross above.

In all life's struggles guide our way,
our choice reflect your love each day.
If facing darkness be our path
help us embrace the cross at last.

Eulogies (Peter, Mary Magdalene)

Peter (with tight control, which occasionally cracks):

Lying there is Jesus my friend, my teacher, a healer and miracle worker, the person I believed to be the Messiah. He turned my life upside down – not just my life but the lives of many. He came into my life about three years ago when he called Andrew and me to leave our nets and follow him: to become fishers of men – we just went, not knowing where it would lead.

What a rag-tag group we were, the twelve he called: not the usual clever and intellectual disciples chosen by a rabbi. We were just ordinary folk – fishermen, a tax collector – searching for something that Jesus seemed to know about.

Jesus turned water into wine, he cast out demons, he healed people – my own mother-in-law was one of the first. He fed five thousand; he calmed the storm, he walked on water … and kept me afloat when my faith weakened. He taught about the Kingdom, and a different way of relating.

He read the scriptures and taught with a new authority that really upset the Pharisees and Sadducees. They were always trying to trip him up with their clever questions but he always had an answer for them … Do you remember the question about paying taxes? They really thought they had caught him out – I shall never forget his answer. Taking a Roman coin he asked them whose head was on it. 'Caesar's,' they said … 'Give to Caesar what is his, and give to God what is his,' answered Jesus.

Last week we came to Jerusalem with people celebrating Jesus – lining his way with palms, shouting with joy – and now he lies dead; crucified with common criminals. Only last night we celebrated the Passover. It was so special. Jesus insisted on washing all our feet; I didn't want him to but he insisted – he even washed the feet of Judas ... During the meal he took bread and wine, blessed them and offered them to us all, saying they were his body and blood, broken for us ... now I understand what he meant.

He told us, yet again, to love God, our neighbours and one another. He predicted that one of us would betray him – how could Judas lead the High Priest's guards to the garden where Jesus was at prayer? But he also told me that I would deny him. Not just once but three times, and I did ... How could I? I'm so sorry, Jesus ...

We did try to defend him, but he stopped us. He even healed the High Priest's slave whose ear was cut off – and we all ran away, all deserted him, leaving him in the hands of his enemies. There followed a trial, if that's what you could call it. He was falsely accused, yet did not defend himself. I could not stand by the cross as John and the women did: I failed him once again ...

I really *do* believe that he was the Messiah – his new teachings, his miracles, his authority, and that strange experience on the mountain when we saw him with Moses and Elijah and heard the voice of God – he must be the Messiah.

I don't know where we go from here, all seems lost; but I am changed. I am not the same person who met Jesus three years ago. Jesus has changed me for ever ...

Mary Magdalene (with strong emotion):

I cannot believe that I am standing here, or that this dreadful day has ended like this. Jesus – that tender, loving, compassionate man, dying on the cross as we watched. Yet as we watched – horrified – we were hoping against all hope that something would happen, that he would not die. But here he is, dead, and soon we bury him.

Jesus meant everything to me – I loved him ... still love him – with all my heart. He rescued me from the horrors of mental illness – he rescued many from illness and gave us *life* again. It did not matter to him who you were, or what your status was: he offered life and healing; he said it showed his Father's love. He taught us – and oh how good it was to meet a rabbi who would teach us women. He taught us all about God's way of being family, being kin, and all – all were included. No one was dirty scum, sinner beyond forgiveness, too poor, too sick, all of us were included in God's Kingdom.

His way of laughing with us, his smile, his jokes that made us realise how radical, how life-changing his teaching was. Like the one about turning the other cheek so if someone was going to hit you, they had to hit you as an equal – I remember the smile going round the crowd as we realised that one!

We believed he was the Messiah, and he did save us, he did. He saved me and made me whole again, but I do not see how … I do not understand … but we who followed him will always love him – and we will try, Jesus, we will try to live as you taught us to. Thank you so much for all you have given us.

Lament: Sung by a choir (Pergolesi's 'Stabat Mater' works well, but choose one to suit your choir or singing group.)

Lamenting the crucified of our time

The Red List

Creation's song
laments the passing
of Holdridge's toad;
baiji; Tasmanian wolf.
Sings a mourning song
for black mamo;
passenger pigeon; Carolina parakeet.
Grieves the loss
of *undulata delissea*;
galipea ossana; Hawaii chaff flower.
Grieves the loss,
endless the names
that sob through song.
From tiny insect to great mammal,
creation's celebrities
wounded to death.

Then beseeching, pleading,
the music crescendos:
Protect the threatened black lion tamarin;
the fishing cat; Iberian lynx.
Shelter the endangered blue-throated macaw;
the mallee emu-wren; the araripe manakin.
Conserve the disappearing moon trefoil;
the jellyfish tree; *rafflesia magnifica.*

Care for the earth
and the skies above,
restore the harmony
of creation's song ...

A lament for earthquake and tsunami victims

The plates of the planet move,
the rocks crack, the earth heaves,
the sea roars.
And humans die:
swiftly as they are crushed or drowned;
slowly as they lie waiting for water,
waiting for rescue.

We lament their loss of life,
grieve their deaths,
wail at the waste,
wish things were different.
For they are gone:
dead to family and friends,
dead all the gifts they offered.
God receive them.

God receive them;
God hold them;
God hear our cry ...

Listen: An Amnesty International banned radio advertisement

Listen … can you hear it? … it's the sound of the hillsides and fields of Rwanda where in their hundreds of thousands the dead lie silent.

Listen … it's the sound of fear in neighbouring Burundi where people are praying that the killing machetes will not come their way.

Listen … it's the stored up, concentrated silence of prisoners locked away for years for a thing they once thought, or believed, or were.

Listen … it's the only message there will ever be from the disappeared, snatched by death squads, never to be seen or heard from by their families again.

Listen … it's the silence of the small room after the torturers have left.

Listen … it's the silence in the councils of great nations when these difficult subjects are left unmentioned.

Listen … it's the silence of ordinary, decent people who think these things have nothing to do with them, and that they can do nothing to help.

Listen … deep inside yourself. What do you hear?

Break the silence.

Prayers

Leader: Can we hear God say?:
'My people, what wrong have I done to you?
What good have I not done for you?
Listen to me.'

Give us grace to listen, precious God,
for Jesus came and we did not recognise him.
The warmth of your love is among us,
and we do not recognise him.

Abba, hear our prayer:

ALL: A sung kyrie (e.g. 'Kyrie Maurs' from *We Walk His Way*, John L.
        Bell, Wild Goose Publications)

Leader: Let us be with you wherever you are crucified today,
        wherever human will crosses the will of God.
        Where the will to violence crosses God's will for peace.
        Where lying and corruption cross God's will for truth.
        Where greed and possessiveness cross the responsible use
        of God's plenty.
        Where ugliness and disease cross the will of God for beauty
        and well-being.
        Where we live not for others but for ourselves.
        There let us find you, racked on the cross,
        and there let us be with you and share your pain.
        Abba, hear our prayer:

ALL: (Sung kyrie)

Leader: Holy God,
        holy and loving,
        holy and vulnerable …

        Abba, hear our prayer:

ALL: (Sung kyrie)

Leader: As our Saviour taught us, so we pray:

ALL: Lord's Prayer

Ending

*The cross is covered reverently with the purple cloth. As people leave (in silence
and in their own time), they can throw leaves on the coffin/tomb space if they
wish. Choose some suitable quiet music to be played while people are leaving
or remain in prayer.*

Sources and acknowledgements:

'Contemplate Christ's sacrifice' – © Chris Polhill

'The Red List' – © Chris Polhill (See www.iucnredlist.org)

'Peter's eulogy' – © Denise Youngs. Used by permission

'Mary Magdalene's eulogy' – © Chris Polhill

'Earthquake victims' – © Chris Polhill

Listen, An Amnesty international banned radio advertisement, from *The Living Spirit*, edited by Margaret Hebblethwaite, Canterbury Press. Used by permission of Amnesty International www.amnesty.org.uk, author unknown.

Prayers – © Debra Dyson. Used by permission

A Good Friday liturgy of
Bible readings and prayers
(John 17–19)

Jan Sutch Pickard

Welcome

Call to worship: John 17:1, 4–5

Song: 'There is a green hill far away', CH4 380

Prayer of approach:

God of community, we gather in your presence in this safe place. We are your straying sheep and your loved children. We gather to hear the story of that love embodied in Jesus and expressed through his death, on a cross outside a city wall. We gather to reflect, to remember and to sing of that love. May we know your presence in this time of sharing, in the story, in our silence, in our song …

Reading 1: John 17: 6–9a, 20–23

Song: 'My song is love unknown' (verses 1 and 2), CH4 399

Reading 2: John 18:1–11

Prayer B:

Forgive us, patient God, we are so quick to strike out; like Peter, ready to take offence, trigger-happy. We may think we're in the right, but, to defend ourselves – or simply to make our point – we hurt others. Often it's sharp words, not swords. But that's never your way, not as Jesus lived it. Peter thought he should defend his friend. But Jesus told him: 'Put away your sword. This is the cup God has given me. Shall I not drink it?' On that night, in dark Gethsemane, Jesus took the cup of obedience to God's will, of non-violence, of suffering, for our sakes. Amen

Reading 3: John 18:12–14, 19–24

Prayer C:

Jesus, you didn't go behind people's backs; you didn't gossip, you didn't mutter in corners. You spoke out for all to hear. You taught what you believed – and you lived it: God's inclusive love, that saves sinners, learns from children and turns the world upside down. The people in power found that too dangerous. They arrested you and hit you in the face. They were face to face with God's love – and they didn't recognise it. Help us to hear your voice and see your face in those around us. Amen

Reading 4: John 18:15–18, 25–27

Prayer D:

Forgive us, God – we call ourselves your friends but we keep on letting you down. Sometimes we're afraid of what people think, even ashamed to be called Christians. Peter denied you – and the cock crowed three times. We imagine his shock and his shame when he came to his senses. And we pray that even when we are afraid, we will keep faith. Amen

Reading 5: John 18:28–40

Prayer E:

What is truth? Jesus came to witness to the truth. What is truth? The truth was in Jesus, and for some that truth was hard to take. What is truth? God, help us to keep asking, to keep open minds so that the truth of your love for each one of us can enter in. Amen

Reading 6: John 19:1–16a

Prayer F:

God help us: it's so easy to go with the crowd, not to stand out, to say what everyone says: 'We want Barabbas …' 'We have no king but Caesar … "Crucify!' We blame those people in a crowd in Jerusalem 2000 years ago. But if we had been there – wouldn't we have done the same?

Song: 'My song is love unknown' (verses 3, 4, 5), CH4 399

Reading 7: John 19:16b–22

Prayer G:

Pilate was a powerful ruler – and yet he gave in to political arguments and a mob who shouted for blood. Pilate was a weak man – and yet he got one thing right: he wrote that Jesus was a king. A king with no power at all. A man discarded, on the town rubbish tip, dying like a criminal on a shameful cross. And yet here was a man filled with the power of God to change the world. Come, Jesus, change us. Come, Jesus, reign in our hearts. Amen

Song: 'Here hangs a man discarded', CH4 385

Reading 8: John 19:23–24

Prayer H:

O God, your Gospel is full of signs. The seamless robe – work of human hands – which the soldiers couldn't tear (so they gambled for it instead). Seamless, one piece, it reminds us of the way we belong together, with each other and with believers down the centuries. Each connection we make brings us nearer to you. We know that Jesus was a carpenter who died on a wooden cross – the work of human hands – and so we pray:

Christ the Master Carpenter, who, at the last, through wood and nails, shaped our whole salvation, wield well your tools in the workshop of your world, so that we who come rough-hewn to your bench may here be fashioned to a truer beauty of your hand. We ask it for your own name's sake. Amen[1]

Reading 9: John 19: 25-27

Period of silence

Song: 'Were you there when they crucified my Lord?', CH4 403

Reading 10: John 19: 28–30

Prayer I:

Living Lord, living Word, living Water, we know that in many places in our world people are thirsty. They suffer from drought; they walk miles to collect water; what little water they have is polluted and makes them sick. Forgive us when we take plentiful clean water for granted. May we never waste it – and may we find ways to give practical help to those without. But also remind us, God, that in Jesus you shared our human lives – and our suffering. You knew what it was to be weary, in pain and overwhelmed with thirst. You understand our deepest need. Thank you, thank you for being there for us. Amen

Song: 'O sacred head sore wounded', CH4 382

Reading 11: John 19: 31–37

Prayer of intercession:

Compassionate God, as we remember Jesus, whose love for humanity brought him to the cross, we remember the world for which he died. We remember the seamless fabric of creation, which we are doing our best to tear; gambling for its possession – felling forests, burning fossil fuels, gouging out opencast mines, polluting the rivers, over-fishing the seas – we pray for forgiveness for what we are doing to your world.

We remember people who are suffering from drought and other natural disasters *(name countries, people)*, praying that the response of nations will be swift and compassionate.

We remember places and nations where there is conflict *(name countries, situations)*, remembering the conflict in our own nation – the sharp divisions between rich and poor, the crisis of confidence in those in power. We pray for a fair distribution of resources, and compassionate care for the weakest in our own society. We remember conflicts very close to home, recognising when we have a part in them, praying for healing.

And we remember those we know who are suffering now, in body, mind or spirit. We believe in a mystery: just as Jesus shared our mortality and pain as he died on the cross, so you are with those who suffer now, and your wounded hands stretch out with healing and hope. Thank you, God.

Lord's Prayer

Reading 12: John 19: 38–42

Song: 'My song is love unknown' (verses 6, 7), CH4 399

Blessing

'Blessed are those who mourn, for they shall be comforted.'
So now, as we stand by the cross, may God –
who, in Jesus, shared human life and death –
comfort and bless each one of us.
May we know that whatever we have done, we are forgiven;
whatever is happening in our lives, God is with us;
whoever we are, God loves us.
Go, and live in the hope of resurrection,
now and always.
Amen

Note:

1. Based on 'Prayer from the Iona Community', from *Iona Abbey Worship Book*, Wild Goose Publications, 2001

What does it mean
to be obedient to God?
Worship and drama for Good Friday

Tim Aldred

As folk come in they pick up a stone from a basket. A cross is set up as a focal point with a basket of candles nearby (enough for everyone).

Introduction:

Leader:

'Obedience' can be a word that jars. It can make us think of powerful people demanding unquestioning loyalty from their subordinates, enforced with threats. So when Jesus is described as being 'obedient unto death', we might cast God in the same mould – as a distant, cruel dictator. But this is not the case. Jesus was being obedient to the love and truth that comes from God.

This service explores what it meant for Jesus – and means for ourselves – to be obedient to God, and the times when following the light of God's Spirit brings us face to face with pain and suffering: face to face with the cross.

Welcome:

As we meet together, we remember the words of Saint Paul, who urged Christians in the town of Philippi to: *'Have the same mindset as Christ Jesus.'*

So let us invite God to be present in our minds, in our hearts and in our worship now ...

Opening prayer:

O God, we come to you this morning with joy.
THANK YOU FOR THE SUNLIGHT OF SPRING
AND FOR THE GOOD THINGS IN OUR LIVES.

We come to you this morning with sadness.
WE ARE SORRY FOR OUR COMPLACENCY IN THIS SUFFERING WORLD
AND FOR THE WRONG IN OUR LIVES.

We come this morning with hope:
THAT YOUR KINGDOM WILL COME ON EARTH AS IN HEAVEN.

We come as we are:
TRUSTING THAT YOU TAKE US AS WE ARE.

Happy or sad, calm or stressed, successful or failing ...
WE ARE HERE TO WORSHIP YOU.
COME, HOLY SPIRIT.
BE WITH US NOW.

Bible reading: Philippians 2:1–11

Drama:

Narrator: What does it mean to be obedient to God?

For God is not a stern overlord, laying down cruel rules and regulations for folk to toe the line on pain of punishment. Jesus himself told us that God demands no such a thing.

So what does it mean to be obedient to God? To be obedient to God's Spirit of truth, mercy and love?

George and Sam

(Setting: a very smart office. Sam is sitting at his/her desk, reading some papers ... Sound of someone knocking on the door.)

Sam: Come in! *(George enters.)* Hi, George, good to see you.

George: Hi, Sam. Sam, do you have a moment?

Sam: Sure, no worries – I'm always keen to hear from the hallowed halls of the Wealth Management Department! You're doing something right, by the look of your last set of results!

George: Well, Sam, I've got a problem with a client.

Sam: Oh, clients! Or as I like to call them, punters – what's the story? Not happy with the fees? Tell you what, do what I do – bung them tickets for Ascot and they'll soon come 'round.

George: No, it's not that, Sam, it's just that one of them has asked for something, well, just a bit unusual.

Sam: Oho! Tell me more.

George: Well, this particular client isn't keen on paying their tax bill.

Sam: Who is George, who is? And that's what your department's for, isn't it?

George: No, Sam, I mean *really* not keen. His exact words were: 'Can't you set me up with one of those numbered accounts in the Caribbean? I really *don't* need the taxman's sticky paws on this little stash.'

Sam: Ah, I see, one of *those* clients.

George: Yes, one of *those* clients.

Sam: So, I'm guessing you've never done it before? It's pretty straight-forward: just speak to the 'special circumstances' team – your fis-cally shy client will be banking offshore before you can say 'customs and excise', and you'll see a nice bonus at the end of the quarter, I've no doubt.

George: The thing is, Sam, I don't think I can do that.

Sam: Stuff and nonsense, nothing to it.

George: No, Sam, I mean … it's just … wrong. I'd be doing something immoral. Illegal even.

Sam   *(bursts out laughing):* George, you're a WEALTH MANAGEMENT CONSULTANT! What do you think we're here for? Our job is to hide the loot and trouser the fee! Look, it's the real world, everyone does it, this is how you pay your mortgage. Sort it out, George – and sharpish, or you'll not be getting a bonus, you'll be getting a P45.

          (Freeze)

Narrator: Lord, it is hard. Those who speak up for what is right can lose friends, their career and status …

Charlie and the bullies

(Two children are pushing a third around, calling her names.)

Bullies: Weirdo! Look at her hair! Urrrgh – spots. Disgusting. What a spotty, disgusting weirdo! Who was your mum then, a toad or something? Yeah, bet your mum was a toad.

(Charlie rushes in and stands between the children.)

Charlie: Stop it, stop it now, leave Mary alone.

Bullies *(amused)*: Ooh, look at Charlie, sticking up for the weirdo! You like weirdos do you, Charlie? You're a weirdo too, are you? Like toads? Get lost toad-lover!

Charlie *(standing his ground)*: *You* get lost! You can't treat people like this!

Bullies: Oh yeah? Well, see how you like it yourself. *(They start to advance on Charlie.)*

(Freeze)

Narrator: Lord, it is hard. Those who step in to protect the weak suffer insults and violence themselves …

Shahida and Nabeel

Shahida is looking worried. Nabeel enters; they hug or hold hands.

Shahida: Nabeel, thank goodness you're safe. I heard the gunfire and I didn't know what to think.

Nabeel: I'm sorry I was so long. I had to avoid the main roads – I didn't want any of the soldiers to stop me. Shahida, there was an announcement. From the new mayor … And it's not good news.

Shahida: The new mayor? What announcement? Tell me, Nabeel.

Nabeel: Look at this leaflet – they're all over town. It's about people like us – our religion. There's an ultimatum.

Shahida: What do you mean? Let me see! *(reads)*. Oh no! This can't be true!

Nabeel: It is, Shahida. We've got a terrible choice to make.

Shahida: But, Nabeel, they demand that we renounce our faith – to deny the faith of our mother and father. Or – or what?

Nabeel: Or leave. Leave our home – our jobs – our friends.

Shahida: But go where? Everything we have is here. We'd have nothing, nothing at all. Nabeel, could we not just say the words? Tell them what they want to hear? We'd know in our hearts what's really true.

Nabeel: But Shahida, how could we? Our faith is not just words to me, or to you – I see it in your face when you pray. How can we deny the good God who is with us, day by day?

Shahida: But where is he now, Nabeel, when we need him most? O, God! My God! Why have you forsaken us?

       (Freeze)

Narrator: Lord, it is hard. Those who are true to you can face cruelty, suffering, and even death …

Jesus and Martha

Martha is washing up in the kitchen; Jesus joins her.

Jesus: Do you need a hand, Martha?

Martha: I wouldn't mind, Jesus, thank you. Would you dry please? It's nice to have a houseful, but it makes for a lot of washing-up.

       Jesus grabs a tea towel and starts to dry.

(Martha bursts out): Are you really back going to Jerusalem? After what happened in the temple! Chasing all the traders out. You've made powerful enemies.

Jesus: I must, Martha.

Martha: Must! Must you really? You men are all the same. Putting yourself and others in danger! And for what? You could head off for a while, let everything cool down. Teach in the local synagogue. Heal minds, bodies and souls. Like you've done with me, Mary and Lazarus. It would be a good life. An important life.

Jesus: I know. But I have to be obedient to my Father.

Martha: There you go again. More of your spiritual riddles. Sometimes I wish you'd just speak in plain Aramaic.

Jesus: OK, Martha, if you insist. You remember when your brother was close to death. What would you have done to save his life at that moment?

Martha   *(holds up a wooden spoon):* I'd have broken down the walls of Pilate's fortress with this spoon, if it would have made any difference.

Jesus: That love you have for your brother – it's the same love that my Father has for all his children. The beggars, the prostitutes, the merchants, the soldiers – even the religious zealots. The same love.

And when I look into his children's eyes I want them to know that love too. None of them can see it, but it is staring them in the face. They are like … like …

Martha: Sheep without a shepherd?

Jesus: You know, that's not a bad line, Martha.

Martha: So, you have to go?

Jesus: No, I don't. But it is where love calls me.

(Freeze)

Narrator: Lord, it is so hard. In your presence, there is life in all its fullness. And yet being true to your Holy Spirit within us can lead to the cross.

Affirmation of faith:

Leader: Lord, being obedient to your Father's Spirit led you to the cross.

All: Our Lord Jesus,
you refused to deny God's Spirit of grace, mercy and love.
Therefore God has exalted you to the highest place
and yours is the name above every name.

Jesus, we kneel *(or stand)* before you.
We acknowledge that you are Lord,
to the glory of God the Father.

Prayer before action:

Let us pray ...

Lord, we carry many burdens:

the cruel words said
the humiliations inflicted
the regrets in our relationships
the failures in our lives
the damage to your creation
the violence of our world
our fear of the future
our fear of those who are different
the hope that has been lost ...

Lord, we lay our burdens down at the foot of the cross.
We cannot bear them.
We cannot carry them further.
We lay them down at the foot of the cross.

Lord we carry your light within us:

your compassion
your kindness
your gentleness
your wisdom
your courage
your strength
your joy
your eternal love
your still small voice ...

Lord, we are here at the foot of the cross.
Empty us of all the rubbish.
Fill us, Lord, in a new way.

May your Spirit live within us.
May we be obedient to the path you light before us.

Action (laying stones at the foot of the cross):

Folk are invited to come and place their stone at the foot of the cross; and then to pick up a candle from the basket: representing the light of God's Spirit with us (have someone nearby to light each person's candle, or pass the light along).

Prayer (said all together while holding lighted candles):

Jesus Christ is Lord, to the glory of God the Father.
Lord, with your help, I promise to be true to your Spirit within me.
Amen

Blessing

Note:

A big thank you to the folk of St Mary's Shortlands for all their support in developing this material, and much else besides, Tim Aldred

Living Easter
An all-age Communion for Easter

Nancy Cocks

Opening responses or opening prayer

Song: an Easter song on the gentler side

The Easter story begins: Matthew 28:1–2

After the sabbath, as the first day of the week was dawning, Mary Magdalene and the other Mary went to see the tomb where Jesus had been laid. And suddenly there was a great earthquake; for an angel of the Lord, descending from heaven, came and rolled back the great stone that had sealed the tomb – and sat on it.

Reflection (feeling Easter):

How many people here have ever felt an earthquake?

Sometimes an earthquake just shakes gently for a second or two.

Maybe the dishes rattle but nothing more.

Other times, a strong earthquake shakes buildings, cracks them open and causes a lot of damage.

You'll see pictures on the news when a big earthquake happens.

But whether it's big or small, whenever you feel an earthquake, even a small one, you remember that people are not really in charge of the earth.

There are powers in the earth stronger than we are.

So at Easter, we feel a power stronger than we are; a power as strong as an earthquake.

We feel the power of God's angel rolling the huge stone away from the mouth of the cave where they'd buried Jesus.

It takes a power as strong as an earthquake to move big boulders!

At Easter we feel power beyond our control.

We feel the power of new life shake our hearts with excitement because something mysterious is happening; something that brings joy back to our hearts today because we know God's amazing power is still at work in the world.

Prayer:

God of Easter mystery, we know the Easter story but we do not understand how things happened as that day dawned. Help us trust that your power is at work in the world even when we can't see an angel for ourselves. Fill our hearts with joy as we sing our songs for Jesus, risen by your power today!

Sung response: Verse one of 'In the bulb there is a flower', by Natalie Sleeth, Hope Publishing, CH4 727

The Easter story continues: Matthew 28:2–5a

An angel of the Lord came and rolled back the stone and sat on it. His appearance was like lightning, and his clothing white as snow. For fear of him the guards shook and became like dead men. But the angel said to the women, 'Do not be afraid.'

Reflection (seeing Easter):

We've all seen lightning flash, right?

When lightning comes at night it makes the dark as bright as day for a second or two.

At Easter, God's angel was even brighter than lightning at night.

His clothes were so dazzling, it was like sunshine bouncing off a field of pure white snow.

That angel was so bright, all those Roman soldiers guarding Jesus' grave were afraid.

They froze in fear and looked stiff and pale as if they were dead.

Saint Matthew is making fun of the soldiers – big strong men with swords, now shaking in their boots.

Not so powerful any more!

Try to picture the scene from Easter morning in your imagination: the flashing angel; the huge stone rolled on its side; soldiers with faces white with fear and Jesus' women friends standing there, wondering what happened.

It's meant to make us smile.

God is turning things upside down – so the sad frowns from Good Friday, the day Jesus died, have turned upside down, too, and become glad smiles of surprise.

That flashy angel turns to Jesus' friends and says, 'Do not be afraid.'

Easter is amazing – so don't be afraid of its flash of lightning!

Easter lightning is the power of God's love bursting into the world to light up any dark corner and show us, with God's power, nothing can make us afraid.

Prayer:

God of Easter wonder, Jesus' friends saw amazing things that day – the angel, the dazzling light, the empty tomb. Where will we see Easter this year? In an angel who brings us unexpected good news? In the smile that lights up the eyes of an old friend? Show us Easter, O God, in signs of new life all around us, surprising us, in Jesus' name.

Sung response: verse 2 of 'In the bulb there is a flower'

The Easter story continues: Matthew 28:5–10

The angel said to the women, 'I know that you are looking for Jesus who was crucified. He is not here; for he has been raised, as he said. Come, see the place where he lay. Then go quickly and tell his disciples, "He has been raised from the dead. And indeed he is going ahead of you to Galilee; there you will see him." This is my message for you.'

So they left the tomb quickly with fear and great joy, and ran to tell his disciples. Suddenly Jesus met them and said, 'Greetings!' And they came to him, took hold of his feet, and worshipped him. Then Jesus said to them, 'Do not be afraid; go and tell my brothers to go to Galilee; there they will see me.'

Hearing Easter: the rooster's story:

(For this drama you will need three voices: a rooster, Mary, a narrator. The rooster should play up the crowing!)

Rooster: Cock-a-doodle-doo! What a grrrreat day!

Narrator: The old rooster scratched the dirt, looking for a grub to eat.

Rooster: Errrrrly bird gets the worm! But Mary was up earlier than I was today. Left the courtyard before dawn. I could smell the spices she carried. Cluck, cluck! Going to tend to Jesus' body.

Narrator: The rooster nodded sadly as he studied the ground.

Rooster: Too bad about Jesus. Died on Friday. I'll miss him around the yard. Such a friendly sort!

Narrator: The rooster scratched around the yard as dawn spread its light. Suddenly Mary appeared, running, breathing hard.

Rooster: Brawk! Mary!

Mary: Peter! I must find Peter! Rooster, have you seen Peter this morning?

Rooster: Stay away from Peter, Mary. He threw a stone at me when I crowed on Frrriday. Just doing my job and he hurled a rock right at my beak.

Narrator: The rooster cocked its head.

Rooster: It was the morning Jesus died. Guess Peter was pretty upset.

Mary: *(sighing)* Rooster, we were all upset when Jesus died. Peter most of all. He let Jesus down, you know. So he'll be amazed this morning. I must find him.

Narrator:	Mary started to knock on all the doors in the village square.
Rooster:	Brawk! Mary, that's my job – to wake up people still in bed. What news can't keep until everyone's up and about?
Narrator:	The rooster flapped its way to the top of the courtyard wall to watch what was happening. Soon Peter and John came outside, rubbing the sleep from their eyes. Mary was waving her hands, pointing down the road.
Rooster:	Cluck, cluck. Listen to that woman flap her gums! Did you hear what she said? That Jesus is gone from his grave. Strrrange morning!
Narrator:	The rooster hopped down from the wall to hunt up a little more breakfast. Mary hurried past, her face glowing.
Mary:	Out of my way, old rooster! He is risen.
Rooster:	Who's an 'old rrrooster'? Of course, everyone has risen. I've been on the job. Er-er-er-er-rroooo! There. That should wake even the late sleepers.
Narrator:	But Mary kept dancing around the courtyard, shouting:
Mary:	He is risen! Jesus is alive! I saw him this very morning.
Narrator:	She hammered on shutters still closed to the rising sun.
Mary:	Come on, sleepyheads. Jesus is risen. Get a move on!
Narrator:	The rooster cocked its head in surprise.
Rooster:	Jesus is risen? Did I crow loud enough to wake the dead this morning?
Narrator:	Peter and John were excited too. 'Come on, people. Jesus wants to meet us in Galilee. Let's get going!' Mary ran up to embrace them, laughing.
Mary:	So you *do* believe the news.

Narrator: The rooster began to flap his wings.

Rooster: No wonder it's such a grrreat day. Come on, Peter. Come on, John!

Narrator: The rooster pecked at their toes.

Rooster: Jesus is risen. Don't just stand there! Get up and go!

Narrator: Peter smiled. 'Sorry about Friday morning, rooster. But watch those toes or I'll aim another stone at that beak! So let's get going!'

Worship leader: The first Easter was full of the sounds of joy, as Jesus' friends began to discover that he had risen from the dead. Even that old rooster crowed with joy!

So at Easter, we continue to make sounds of joy in the songs we sing – to waken our hearts with God's love and tell everyone the good news: Jesus is risen. And God can make all things new!

Prayer:

God of Easter Joy, we're glad today that Jesus is risen from the dead! Help us to feel the same joy his friends felt that first Easter Day. Help us get a move on to tell the world that Jesus Christ is risen today! Amen

The next chapter of Easter: Matthew 28:16–20

Now the eleven disciples went to Galilee, to the mountain to which Jesus had directed them. When they saw him, they worshipped him; but some doubted. And Jesus came and said to them, 'All authority in heaven and on earth has been given to me. Go therefore and make disciples of all nations, baptising them in the name of the Father and of the Son and of the Holy Spirit, and teaching them to obey everything that I have commanded you. And remember, I am with you always, to the end of the age.'

Living Easter:

This part of the service requires sprouted bulbs, and a couple of plain bulbs. In our church, we'd planted bulbs and tried to force them to bloom at Easter. Blooms were nowhere to be seen but the bulbs had sprouted enough to show a few centimetres of green. If you're a better gardener, perhaps you can plant the bulbs early enough to have them bloom. Adjust the conversation as needed.

What do you see in the pot?

We planted tulip bulbs in this dirt back in February.

Here's what they looked like before we planted them – brown and papery, pretty ugly, if you ask me.

Now this pot isn't blooming yet.

We would have had to plant the bulbs last autumn to have them bloom for Easter.

But that's the interesting thing about bulbs.

You plant them just as winter is coming and they start to grow slowly, slowly, slowly while everything else in the world is sound asleep for the winter.

Then in spring, bulbs are the first things to grow in our gardens.

They remind us that God's Spirit is always at work, helping us grow even when we're not watching; bringing new life from things that looked dried up or dead.

Like the song says, *in every bulb there is a flower waiting to be born.*

In every person, there is something interesting and beautiful waiting to grow up and bloom so the world can see who we are and what we can do for God's sake.

God's power is at work in every growing thing; and at Easter we trust that God's power is so strong, not even death can stop it!

God brings new life to the world in everything and everyone who lives in ways to praise God in Jesus' name.

Sung response: verse 3 of 'In the bulb there is a flower'

We give our gifts to God in Jesus' name …

The Offering

If your Easter service does not include Communion then move to the Prayers of the people after the Offering, following the themes of the service: have sections about what God would have an Easter people see and hear, followed by a section seeking God's courage and strength to live Easter in response to what we see and hear in God's world.

Tasting Easter, an invitation to the Table:

Jesus told us that people will come from east and west
and from north and south
to sit at the table in God's kingdom.
This is God's table.
Here we celebrate with Jesus, who is risen to join us,
as we taste bread and wine in his name.
These gifts of his table are for all those who love him
and for all who want to love him more.
Today taste Easter and know that God is good!

An Easter or Communion song (one which is more rousing, e.g. 'The Day of Resurrection', various songbooks)

The story of our Easter Table:

O God, on this joyful Easter Day we open our hearts to you.
We have seen the power of your love roll away the stone from Jesus' grave.
We have heard his friends shout with joy once they heard his voice again.
And so we join our voices with all God's creatures high and low,
with all Jesus' friends from long ago, and here and now,
to sing your praises:

Sung response: a Sanctus the children know, or one sung cantor/response style

Receive our joyful praise today, Lord Jesus.
You rose from the dead to show us
that there are new possibilities for us and our lives, too.
Even when we're sad or discouraged and forget your love,
you don't turn away from us.
You open up your arms to catch us in a hug.
You invite us to share this meal with you
so that we may taste your love and feel it through and through.
Lord Jesus, on this happy Easter Day,
we raise our voices to sing our joy out loud:

Sung response: an Acclamation the children can sing, or one sung cantor/
response style

Holy Spirit, you make new life rise in us and around us.
Breathe upon us now and upon this bread and wine
so we can taste the love of Christ Jesus.
As this bread and wine become a part of us, Lord Jesus,
make us a part of you and your family everywhere.
Help us trust that all things will work together for good,
through the power of God's love that raised you from the dead,
the power of the love we share today in your name.
Amen

Breaking the bread and pouring the cup:

The Bread of Life. The cup of Joy. Taste and know that God is good.

Take God's blessing with you.

The peace of our Lord Jesus Christ be with you
AND ALSO WITH YOU.

Prayers of the people

A prayer for God to go with us:

Loving God, your love is as close to us as our own hands and feet.
People who need your love are as close to us

as the people beside us, behind us and in front of us.
Send us into your world to love each other, sure that you love us.
Show us where we are needed and how we can make a difference
so that the world sees the new life Jesus wants for everyone.
Help us live for Jesus wherever we go, whatever we do.
Amen

An Easter song (one which proclaims resurrection, for example, 'Jesus Christ is risen today', various songbooks)

Closing responses:

The cross …
WE SHALL TAKE IT.

The bread …
WE SHALL BREAK IT.

The pain …
WE SHALL BEAR IT.

The joy …
WE SHALL SHARE IT.

The Gospel …
WE SHALL LIVE IT.

The love …
WE SHALL GIVE IT.

The light
WE SHALL CHERISH IT.

The darkness
GOD SHALL PERISH IT.

(From *Iona Abbey Worship Book*)

Blessing

That all may dance
A simple liturgy for Pentecost to Trinity Sunday

Chris Polhill

This liturgy is suitable for any time between Pentecost and Trinity Sunday. Use different voices; leave space for folk to pray.

Opening prayer:

May the flame of the Spirit
touch our souls,
the light of Christ's truth
fill our minds,
and the love of the Maker
fill our hearts
as we worship together this day.
AMEN

Bible reading: Acts 2:1–13

Circling prayers:

For these prayers you could have a small group stand in a circle in the centre of the prayer space and fan prayer or dance flags.

Let us pray:

Holy Spirit, we circle the world with the flame of your love,
and pray for peace and justice where there is inequality and war;
for dancing and joy in place of oppression
and the daily grind of poverty *(name places, situations)* …
May all enjoy the feast of life.

Your will be done,
ON EARTH, AS IN HEAVEN.

Lady Wisdom,
we circle this *place/church* with the flame of your love –
and thank you for friends and fun, for gifts and talents.
We pray for your peace in our hearts as we journey along together,
and for a knowledge of your gifts within us.

Your will be done,
ON EARTH, AS IN HEAVEN.

Healing Spirit,
we circle with your blessing all those who will be born today.
Protect and cherish them, loving God …

We circle with your healing love
all those who are enduring illness or disease *(names, situations)* …
Be with them in their suffering, O God …

And we circle with your glorious light,
all those who will die today.
Take them into your arms
and embrace them, O God …

Your will be done,
ON EARTH, AS IN HEAVEN.

Hear our prayers,
and bless us living God.
Hold the secret longings of our hearts
in the mystery of your love,
that the light of the Kingdom
will continue to shine on earth.
AMEN

Silence/pause

Bible reading: 2 Corinthians 13:11–14

Prayer:

May the dance of Christ
be in our souls,
the joy of the Spirit
be in our living,
and the love of the Maker
fill our hearts.
AMEN

Intercessions:

Creator God,
may your outrageous justice,
which offers forgiveness and reconciliation to everyone,
be the choice of our governments and nations:
THAT ALL MAY DANCE IN YOUR KINGDOM TOGETHER.

Jesus our brother,
you welcomed the poor and the despised:
help us to live by your values,
however foolish they seem to those around us.
THAT ALL MAY DANCE IN YOUR KINGDOM TOGETHER.

Holy Spirit,
you comfort and disturb us:
may we dance your wild dance across the boundaries
our culture erects between peoples.
THAT ALL MAY DANCE IN YOUR KINGDOM TOGETHER.

God the Holy Trinity,
you call us into community:
in our churches may we be willing to put aside
any traditions and customs
that stop us from listening to
and loving each other:

HELP US TO LIVE BY YOUR WISDOM.

SET US FREE FROM ALL THAT PREVENTS US
FROM CHOOSING YOUR KINGDOM.

AND HELP US TO RECOGNISE
WHERE YOU ARE AT WORK IN OUR LIVES.

SO MAY YOUR WILL BE DONE,
AND YOUR KINGDOM COME.

Closing responses:

In your world, living God:
WE WILL SING YOUR SONG OF JUSTICE.

In your world, living God:
WE WILL DANCE YOUR DANCE OF PEACE.

In your world, living God:
WE WILL LIVE YOUR WAY OF LOVE.

Blessing:

The song of creation restore you,
the song of justice infuse you,
the song of heaven enlighten you,
and the blessing of the living God,
Father, Son and Holy Spirit,
be with us now and always.
AMEN

Bell, book and candle
A liturgy for St Columba's Day

Jan Sutch Pickard

This is an order of service for use on 9th June, St Columba's Day (the day when Associates of the Iona Community renew their commitment), or at any other appropriate time for your group/congregation. It was compiled during the year of the celebration of the 1450th anniversary of St Columba's arrival in the Isle of Iona.

You will need a leader, a storyteller and two readers; a bell (see notes)[1], a Bible, a large candle and numerous tea-lights.

Welcome

Introduction:

Leader: The title of this service may surprise some of you: Bell, book and candle were used in the past to curse those who had earned the dire disapproval of the church – heretics and wrongdoers. But each of these symbols of religious authority has more positive associations. For the Celtic monks, and for ourselves, they could be symbols of blessing: the blessing of being called; the blessing of hearing and studying God's word; the blessing of being sent out, carrying the Good News. That's what we celebrate today.

The blessing of being called

Gathering song: (such as 'Come all you people')

Ring the bell

Storyteller: The bell calls us to worship, as it called farmers and fishermen centuries ago, in communities on the edge of the known world, blessed by the presence of wandering Celtic monks – many of whom carried a bell as a sign of God's authority[2] and a way of gathering the people.

Opening responses:

> Creator God,
> ever-present like the steady fall of waves on the shore,
> WE HEAR YOUR CALL.
>
> *Ring the bell*
>
> Jesus, Companion,
> as close to us as the beating of our hearts,
> WE HEAR YOUR CALL.
>
> *Ring the bell*
>
> Holy Spirit, on the wind,
> in the heart-stirring music of the wild geese,
> WE HEAR YOUR CALL.
>
> *Ring the bell*

Storyteller: God called Columba from the privilege of a princely family, from the power-base of an Irish monastery, from the solace of kent faces and familiar rituals, to the white martyrdom of exile, to a voyage into the unknown, in a frail *curragh* (coracle) with a few followers, making a series of landfalls as he tried to find the place where God was calling him to begin all over again. There may have been political currents as well as winds and waves that brought them to Iona. But it was still exile. According to legend, the monks came ashore at what is now called Columba's Bay, dragging their *curragh* ashore over the stones, Iona greenstone, now called Columba's tears. Right then, they were turning their backs on Ireland as they followed God's call.

> *Ring bell*

Leader: Let us pray …

> O God,
> we find it hard to let go of all that gives us status or security;
> we cling on to the grief and grievances of the past;
> we talk about putting our trust in you – but we struggle;

we hear your call – but find it hard to take the first step.
You care for our human frailty – forgive us when we fail;
when you call us again, give us courage to follow you.
Amen

Listen to these words from the commitment service in Iona.
Then let us spend a few minutes in silence, thinking about what
they mean to each of us:

Come and follow Jesus,
you who have committed yourselves already,
and you who would like to do so for the first time;
you who have given yourselves to the care of creation
and to the suffering ones of the world,
and you who feel moved by the Spirit
to begin to offer yourselves;
you who have been faithful to your life commitments
and you who have failed.
Come, for our Lord invites us to follow him,
and to make new beginnings in our lives.[3]

Silence

Ring the bell one more time.

Song: (e.g. 'From Erin's shores Columba came' or 'Alone with none but
Thee my God')

The blessing of hearing and studying God's Word

Storyteller: The Celtic monks carried little with them in their wanderings
and voyages, their pilgrimages. Perhaps there was a bell, and
certainly a book. In its own leather satchel would be a precious
copy of the Gospels or the psalms, often written out by their
own hand. They carried this book.

Reader carries a Bible to the centre of the worship space.

And they opened it.

Reader opens the Bible.

For though it was in itself a precious thing, it was also a way of learning about God. So, amid the dazzling decoration of the Book of Kells, we can discern – in Latin, which was then the language of the Church – these words:

Reader 1:   *In principio erat Verbum, et Verbum erat apud Deum, et Deus erat Verbum. Hoc erat in principio apud Deum. Omnia per ipsum facta sunt: et sine ipso factum est.*

Reader 2:   John 1:1–5 (in English)

Storyteller: 'Through him all things came to be.' And for Celtic Christians, the whole world was *'charged with the grandeur of God'*.[4] In storm, snow and days of gentle sunshine, day after day and in the depths of the starry night, intricate and beautiful, powerful and mysterious, another book opened: the 'great book' of God's creation. Within it they carried and read the 'little book' – the Bible – not less important, but simply something that human hands could hold. And the words of the psalms, for instance, held these two books together.

Readers: Read Psalms 8 and 93

Storyteller: Columba and his followers, as part of their austere religious observance, would sometimes stand waist-deep in the swirling sea, chanting the psalms. And a later Church continued at least part of the tradition, with the metrical psalms – though sung on dry land!

Leader: We'll now sing one of the well-known metrical psalms from the *Scottish Psalter* (e.g. 'How excellent in all the earth', Psalm 8; 'All people that on earth do dwell', Psalm 100; 'The Lord's my shepherd, I'll not want', Psalm 23).

Song: (one of the metrical psalms)

Storyteller: And, so that the words would not be lost, the daily work of some monks would be the copying out of scripture, with quill pens and ink from the oak-gall. The story goes that on the day Columba died he was copying these words:

Reader: Psalm 34:1–10

Storyteller: There, on Iona, sustained by the psalms, did people taste and see that God was good? The monks built their cluster of beehive cells, and their little church; they gathered for worship but also honoured God in their daily work, farming on the fertile land of Iona and Tiree, caring for the sick, preaching to the people, copying out the scriptures and welcoming the many guests who made the journey to Iona – seeking advice, absolution, healing, blessing. The person of Abbot Columba and the sanctuary of the monastic 'family' drew people from different walks of life to Iona. There they also experienced the presence of God – as many do today.

Song: 'I bind unto myself today' or 'Christ be beside me' (to the tune 'Bunessan')

During this hymn a large candle is lit in the centre of the worshippers.

Leader: Let us pray …

O God, who gave to your servant Columba
the gifts of courage, faith and cheerfulness,
and sent people forth from Iona
to carry the word of your gospel to every creature:
grant, we pray, a like spirit to your church,
even at this present time.
Further in all things the purpose of our community,
that hidden things may be revealed to us,
and new ways found to touch the hearts of all.
May we preserve with each other sincere charity and peace,
and, if it be your holy will,
grant that this place of your abiding

be continued still to be a sanctuary and a light.
Through Jesus Christ,
Amen[5]

The blessing of being sent out, carrying the Good News

Storyteller: *'A sanctuary and a light'.* But the light was never intended to be
hidden under a basket or in a beehive cell – or in a 12th-century
abbey or a 20th-century reconstruction, or in a youth camp, or
a Centre welcoming pilgrims. It must be seen; it needs to be
carried out from Iona. Ralph Morton, a founding member of the
Iona Community, used to say: *'The Iona experience is meant to be
exported.'* That was true from the beginning: Columba himself
went out on mission from Iona as far as Inverness; he was
involved in the politics of the Kingdom of Dalriada, in what is
now Argyll. Monks from Iona voyaged by coracle among the
islands, as hermits but also as missionaries and priests to local
communities. Later, Aidan travelled as far as Northumbria and
Lindisfarne.

*As each of these 'goings-out' above is mentioned, tea-lights can be
lit from the central candle, and placed round it.*

When people from all over Scotland came as pilgrims to the
shrine of St Columba, in the days of the Celtic monks and later
the Benedictine monastery, they found hospitality, but this little
island couldn't hold all who came, and they went back with
renewed faith to their homes.

More candles are lit.

After the Reformation, when the Abbey lay in ruins, curious
travellers still visited …

Reader: 'We were now treading that illustrious island, which was once
the luminary of the Caledonian regions, whence savage clans
and roving barbarians derived the benefits of knowledge, and
the blessings of religion … That man is little to be envied, whose
… piety would not grow warmer among the ruins of Iona.'[6]

Storyteller: And Dr Johnson and James Boswell went on their way, and shared their experience in print.

Light candles

The Abbey Church was rebuilt more than a hundred years ago, and big pilgrimage groups came from Glasgow – and went back, with warmer piety, to the challenges of city parishes.

Light candles

In the 1930s, George MacLeod started bringing unemployed craftsmen and ministers in training to work on the rebuilding of the abbey quarters and cloister – *'the place of the common life'*. The Iona Community came into being around the rebuilding. But its members could not stay in the sanctuary of the island. They had homes and families to return to. The young ministers were called to work in housing schemes, industrial mission, developing countries. They carried with them the light of their new understanding of community and social justice.

Light candles

And Iona Community members seldom stay for long in Iona – they go back to their work in schools, hospitals, offices; listen to those living in poverty; grapple with the needs and rights of asylum seekers; become Ecumenical Accompaniers on the Separation Barrier between Israel and Palestine; campaign about climate change and a sustainable lifestyle; risk peaceful protest against nuclear weapons at Faslane or Aldermaston: each in their own way carrying the light.

Light candles

Every week in the season, now, people come from all over the world, drawn to Iona. Leaving, they carry within them the light of new understandings of God, of themselves, of the needs of others. The legacy and blessing of Columba, the gift of God.

If we carry lit candles into the world outside these sheltering walls, the wind often blows them out *(possible reference to poem*

'Carrying a candle', see Optional activity). So, as we sing again, you are invited to take an unlit candle from the basket in the centre. Take it with you as you go away from here to the place – home, local church, new place of work, community centre – where God is calling you to be and to shine. Light it there.

Song: 'Christ be our light' or 'We are walking in the light of God'

Blessing:

Leader: And now may kindly Columba guide you
to be an isle in the sea,
to be a hill on the shore,
to be a star in the night,
to be a staff for the weak.
Amen

and/or

May God, who is present in sunrise and nightfall,
and in the crossing of the sea,
guide your feet as you go.

May God, who is with you
when you sit and when you stand,
encompass you with love
and lead you by the hand.

May God, who knows your path
and the places where you rest,
be with you in your waiting,
be your good news for sharing,
and lead you in the way that is everlasting.
Amen[7]

Notes:

1. A cowbell, or maybe an old school bell, will work best to evoke the sound of a Celtic saint's bell: they weren't melodious or tinkling, but had a harsh and urgent sound (see poem 'The bell', Optional activity).

2. After the monks' deaths the bells themselves became objects of veneration, enclosed in shrines of leather and cast metal inset with jewels.

3. Call to commitment, from *Iona Abbey Worship Book*, Wild Goose Publications © Iona Community, 2001

4. Reference to Gerard Manley Hopkins' sonnet 'God's grandeur'

5. Prayer, from *Iona Abbey Worship Book*, Wild Goose Publications, 2001

6. From *A Journey to the Western Islands of Scotland*, by Samuel Johnson

7. Blessings, from *Iona Abbey Worship Book*, Wild Goose Publications, 2001

APPENDIX

Suggested hymns and where they can be found

'All people that on earth do dwell' (Psalm 100) – from *Church Hymnary 4* (CH4), Canterbury Press

'Alone with none but thee my God' (words attributed to St Columba) – found in various collections

'Christ be beside me' (to the tune 'Bunessan') – from *Church Hymnary 4* (CH4), Canterbury Press

'Christ be our light' – from *Church Hymnary 4* (CH4), Canterbury Press

'Come all you people' – from *Church Hymnary 4* (CH4), Canterbury Press, or *Come All You People: Shorter songs for worship*, John L. Bell, Wild Goose Publications

'From Erin's shores Columba came' – from *Love from Below: The seasons of life, the call to care and the celebrating community*, John L. Bell and Graham Maule, Wild Goose Publications

'How excellent in all the earth' (Psalm 8) – from *Church Hymnary 4* (CH4), Canterbury Press

'I bind unto myself today' – from *Church Hymnary 4* (CH4), Canterbury Press

'The Lord's my shepherd, I'll not want' (Psalm 23) – from *Church Hymnary 4* (CH4), Canterbury Press

'We are walking in the light of God' – from *Church Hymnary 4* (CH4), Canterbury Press

OPTIONAL ACTIVITY

*In a workshop in Iona people came up with the following words to
describe St Columba, which were painted, letter by letter, and later
made into a huge banner in the Cloisters: Powerful, Pilgrim, Determined, Penitent, Devoted, Saved by Grace, Prophetic, Charismatic,
Stubborn, Troubled Soul, Magnificent, Driven, Humility, Servant. You
could spend time at an appropriate point in this service discussing with
your neighbours what these words tell you about the man.*

Poems for reflection

The bell

At first, I guessed
that its clangour was the cry of wild geese,
lifting off wet meadows,
resonant in the raw air
of a grey midwinter Sunday;

then I heard it was the dissonant beat
of the Parish Church bell,
rusting on its outdoor perch
at the gable end;

and I thought how it lacks the charm
of a chime of bells from a steeple
or the sonorous tolling of the Abbey bell,
ten minutes to each appointed hour.

But how, as it echoes from the crags,
uncompromising in its demand
that the people come –
with no promise of comfort or beauty –
we maybe hear
the gathering bell of a much older church,
the strange certainties of saints,
the urgency of the wild geese.

Jan Sutch Pickard

Carrying a candle

Carrying a candle
from one little place of shelter
to another
is an act of love.

To move through the huge
and hungry darkness, step by step,
against the invisible wind
that blows for ever around the world,
carrying a candle,
is an act of foolhardy hope.

Surely it will be blown out:
the wind is contemptuous,
the darkness cannot comprehend it.
How much light can this tiny flame shed
on all the great issues of the day?
It is as helpless as a newborn child.
Look how the human hand,
that cradles it, has become translucent:
fragile and beautiful; foolish and loving.
Step by step.

The wind is stronger than this hand,
and the darkness infinite
around this tiny here-and-now flame,
that wavers, but keeps burning:
carried with such care
through an uncaring world
from one little place of shelter to another.
An act of love.

The light shines in the darkness
and the darkness can never put it out.

Jan Sutch Pickard

Beyond the baggage
of fatherhood
A liturgy for Father's Day

David McNeish

Things needed:

– *A wooden cross, or a pinboard with black card stuck in each corner to create a cross-shape in the middle of the board. If it is a large gathering you might want to have more than one cross or pinboard.*

– *Card cut into the shape of individual suitcases (enough for the whole group).*

– *Drawing pins*

– *Strips of towel, approximately 3cmx10cm (charity shops often have old towels: a better environmental and labour-force option than buying cheap new towels)*

Notes:

There are two hosts for this service, one male, one female.

The responses of the prayer of intercession can be spoken or sung (see music: 'Have mercy upon the family of God'). If sung, teach the response before worship begins.

Welcome:

Host 1:   Welcome all daughters of fathers.

Host 2:   Welcome all sons of fathers.

Host 1:   Welcome all for whom father is a wounding word.

Host 2:   Welcome all for whom father is an encouraging word.

Host 1:   Welcome all who are fathers.

Host 2:   Welcome all who wish they were fathers.

Host 1:   Welcome all who wish for better fathers.

Host 1 and 2:   Welcome all …

Prayer of approach:

Host 1:   Let us pray:

Great craftsman of all people,
you are the maker of every one of us.
You gift to us life and laughter and loveliness.
You accompany us through pain and terror and loneliness.

Host 2:   You have fashioned people of every kind and outlook;
made each one of us to be image-bearers:
carriers of divine grace.

Host 1:   Forgive us when we treat our own worth with contempt.
Or judge those around us as unworthy of your love –
the wideness of your mercy is hard to grasp.

Host 2:   Help us to forgive those
who have treated our own worth with contempt;
or have judged us as unworthy of your love,
that we might grasp,
a little more,
the wideness of your mercy.

Host 1:   Great mender of lives,
        we ask your Spirit to be at work

Host 2:   To restore,

Host 1:   Refresh,

Host 2:   Renew.

Host 1:   That in each life

Host 2:   Your life may be revealed.

*Host 1
and 2:*   We ask this in the name of the family of Christ.

        AMEN

Song: 'Gathered for God' (from *Gathered for God*, GIA Publications)

The baggage of fatherhood:

Host 1:   The Bible is an uneasy place to find out about fathers: Abraham
        the Father of faith and the unfaithful husband.

Host 2:   Lot who fathers children with his own daughters.

Host 1:   Jacob whose fatherly favouritism causes jealousy and hatred
        amongst his sons, the brothers of Joseph.

Host 2:   David, the man close to God's heart, who fails to punish his son
        for the rape of his daughter.

Host 1:   Stories of human failure and frailty abound.

Host 2:   Yet Joseph does not abandon Mary when he finds out that she is
        mysteriously pregnant.

Host 1:   Instead he chooses to stay, and raises Jesus as his own son.

Host 2:   And Jesus dares to call God 'Father'. Repeatedly. And describes him as one who is all-loving – and who runs out to embrace us and lead us home.

Host 1:   For some, this is an extraordinary revelation of the heart of God.

Host 2:   For others, it is an uncomfortable reality that tests their faith.

Host 1:   Yet what if we were to lavish love upon our children as God does?

Host 2:   What if fathering has a future beyond the bounds of patriarchal oppression?

Host 1:   Where we can acknowledge the shortcomings in our own experience.

Host 2:   And yet not be tethered by them.

Host 1:   Where we can acknowledge the difficulties of fathering well.

Host 2:   And yet not be restricted by them.

Host 1:   Where we can seek, for ourselves and for those we know,

Host 2:   New expressions of fatherhood, rooted and established in love.

Host 1:   You will find at your seat a piece of card shaped like a suitcase.

Host 2:   This represents the baggage of your own experience.

Host 1:   In a moment some gentle instrumental music will be played. During the music, you are invited to reflect on your own experience of fatherhood:

Host 2:   As a daughter or son.

Host 1:   As someone with or without a father.

Host 2:   What is it about your experience that you still carry with you against your wishes? ...

Host 1:   After the music you will be invited to bring this baggage forward and pin it to the cross:

Host 2:   As a way of giving to God – who accepts and understands all – those things which are a burden to us.

Host 1:   Beside the cross you will find a strip of towel.

Host 2:   This represents the example of Jesus Christ, the man who came not to *be* served but *to* serve.

Host 1:   The towel may seem insignificant next to the baggage.

Host 2:   In some ways it is, as it represents the fragile way of selfless love.

Host 1:   Please take this piece of towel away with you, to help you in praying for those who are fathers, or for yourself.

Host 2:   That the same Spirit of Christ be at work as they, and you, seek to serve God.

Host 1:   I invite you to reflect on your own experience of fatherhood ...

(Gentle instrumental music, live or recorded)

Action:

Host 2:   Please come now and bring your baggage to God ...

   Songs during action: 'Come to me' or 'Come bring your burdens to God', from We Walk His Way *(John L. Bell, Wild Goose Publications), or 'Come and find rest in Christ', from* The Truth that Sets Us Free *(John L. Bell, Wild Goose Publications). It might help to have a few people leading the singing.*

Host 1:   Thank you. May your piece of towel be a reminder of the radical alternative that is the way of Christ.

Prayer of intercession:

This prayer can be spoken, or the responses can be sung (see music: 'Have mercy upon the family of God'). Adapt the prayer to make it topical.

Host 2: Let us ask God for mercy once more ...

Host 1: For Nigerian fathers who desire an education for their daughters,

Host 2: For Nigerian fathers who are opposed to this, we cry to you:

HAVE MERCY UPON THE FAMILY OF GOD.

Host 1: For Syrian fathers whose sons are murdered by a state determined to hold on to power,

Host 2: For Syrian fathers who wield the power of the state, we cry to you:

HAVE MERCY UPON THE FAMILY OF GOD.

Host 1: For Israeli fathers fearful of rocket attacks, whose children must serve in the army,

Host 2: For Palestinian fathers fearful of barriers and checkpoints, whose children cannot inherit their family land, we cry to you:

HAVE MERCY UPON THE FAMILY OF GOD.

Host 1: For fathers gripped by addictions, whose appetites overwhelm their affection,

Host 2: For fathers who have abandoned those for whom they have a duty of care,

Host 1: For fathers who believe the lie that violence is a mark of manhood,

Host 2: And for all their sons and daughters, we cry to you:

HAVE MERCY UPON THE FAMILY OF GOD.

Host 1:   For all fathers seeking to love as God does,

Host 2:   For all fathers recognising the inestimable worth of their children,

Host 1:   For all fathers asking for help to serve as fathers,

Host 2:   And for all their sons and daughters, we cry to you:

HAVE MERCY UPON THE FAMILY OF GOD.

Host 1:   Let us continue in prayerful reflection.

Host 2:   Let us sing together 'Pray through me Christ' *(see music).*

Song: 'Pray through me Christ', by David McNeish

Blessing:

Host 1:   As we leave, let us bless one another.

Host 2:   With the blessing we first receive from God.
WE GO IN PEACE TO SEEK PEACE.
WE GO IN GRACE TO SOW GRACE.
WE GO IN LOVE TO SHARE LOVE –
WHEREVER AND WHENEVER IT IS NEEDED –
AND WE DO NOT GO ALONE.
AMEN

Gentle music

Have mercy upon the family of God

words and music by David McNeish

Pray through me Christ

words and music by David McNeish

In the beginning
A liturgy for Harvest Festival

Joy Mead

At the front of the worship space have a selection of seeds and fruit – as many colours, shapes and sizes as you can find. Begin to pass these around during the first readings.

Opening responses:

For the sweetness of soil
from which we come
and to which we will return
WE GIVE THANKS WITH JOY AND WONDER.

For the openness of air
which we breathe
and sometimes walk upon
WE GIVE THANKS WITH JOY AND WONDER.

For the release of water
that bubbles and streams
and sometimes questions
WE GIVE THANKS WITH JOY AND WONDER.

For the surprise of fire
that kindles and flames,
is fearsome and bold
and sometimes lights up faces
with laughter.
WE GIVE THANKS WITH JOY AND WONDER.

May we see in these elements
our need, our fulfilment
and our belonging.

Song: 'Imagination is a tree', by Fred Kaan, from *The Only Earth We Know*, Stainer and Bell

Readings:

Reader 1: Genesis 1:11–13 (REB):

Then God said, 'Let the earth produce growing things; let there be on the earth plants that bear seed, and trees bearing fruit each with its own kind of seed.' So it was: the earth produced growing things; plants bearing their own kind of seed and trees bearing fruit, each with its own kind of seed; and God saw that it was good.

Reader 2: Genesis 47:19 (REB):

Give us seedcorn to keep us alive, or we shall die and our land will become a desert.

Leader:

Sustainability begins with wonder – the wonder of beginnings, of all life and means of life in tiny seeds, each holding secrets necessary to bear 'its own kind of fruit'.

Poem

The given beauty of it –
inert in my palm
tender, fragile thing
quietly holding
good for all people,
complex and intricate,
storing life and the means
of life.

The silent wonder of it –
Jack in the beanstalk story:
always ready to sprout
while the sower is away;
fairy story; or miracle:
seed, soil, labour, love;
life, death, rebirth,

earth's best gift,
seed of freedom
for all our tomorrows.

Leader:

The continuance of life on earth may depend upon the rekindling of our sense of wonder and our understanding of the beauty of fragile connections.

Seed is not commodity. It is gift to be exchanged freely amongst people. Hope comes in such little things, little acts.

Voice 1:

Farming families in Bangladesh have set up seed banks of traditional varieties, which they call 'community seed wealth centres', and by swapping seeds they bypass commercial seed entirely. This maintains not only their self-reliance but the biodiversity of the world's agricultural resources, and this is happening all over the world. Diversity isn't just interesting – it's essential for continuing life. The slogan of the women in Bangladesh is *'Keep the seed in your hand, sister'*. This resists the trend in modern agriculture towards high yields and fashion foods. It's agri-*culture*: about nurturing the seed and the knowledge of local farmers rather than cash investment.

Voice 2:

All beans have their own Jack in the beanstalk story. They are magic in many different ways. A co-operative on the edge of the Peten Rainforest in northern Guatemala uses the macuna bean as fertiliser. These 'magic' beans are planted between rows of maize and allowed to decompose, making bean manure which leaves the soil visibly richer and substantially increases cereal yields naturally and sustainably.

Leader:

Hope is in the God of small things …

Song: 'The greatness of the small', from *Love from Below*, John L. Bell and Graham Maule, Wild Goose Publications

Prayer:

Leader:

May awe and wonder be sustained within us:
so we are able to see the beauty of the earth as a finite whole,
eternity in tiny seeds,
an understanding of life and death
in the fall of a sparrow.
GOD OF ALL LOVE AND EVERY TRUTH,
HELP US TO LOOK WITH OPEN EYES,
TO SEE WITH OPEN HEARTS.

Leader:

May we be filled with vision and imagination:
so we are able to see how waste and greed in one place
diminishes life in another;
help us to rediscover
the significance and surprise in sharing.
GOD OF ALL LOVE AND EVERY TRUTH,
HELP US TO LOOK WITH OPEN EYES,
TO SEE WITH OPEN HEARTS.

Leader:

May we be filled with compassion and understanding:
so we are open to listening to the hidden people,
whose ancient knowledge and wisdom
could be our hope and salvation.
GOD OF ALL LOVE AND EVERY TRUTH,
HELP US TO LOOK WITH OPEN EYES,
TO SEE WITH OPEN HEARTS.

Leader:

May we be filled with fire and vigour,
anger at short-sighted policies,
cold-blooded economics and heartless trading:
so we may protest greed and the misuse of the earth's resources,
and seek passionately
the just use of our abundant knowledge, skills and resources
to cherish all life.
GOD OF ALL LOVE AND EVERY TRUTH,
HELP US TO LOOK WITH OPEN EYES,
TO SEE WITH OPEN HEARTS.

Leader:

Care and use of seeds and growing food is not agribusiness. It's about reverence. It's agri-*culture*. Seed, plants and future life is more than the means to food. It is the storage place of culture and history, the bearer of immortality. Free exchange of seed involves exchanges of ancient and local wisdom, local understanding of soil and society.

Voice 1:

A Sanskrit text written in about 1500 BCE says: *'Upon this handful of soil our survival depends. Husband it and it will grow our food, our fuel and our shelter and surround us with beauty. Abuse it and the soil will collapse and die, taking humanity with it.'*

The UN's Food and Agriculture Organisation says that, due to the degradation of the world's topsoil, the world on average has just *'60 more years of growing crops'*. In Britain, *Farmers' Weekly* reports *'the UK only has 100 harvests left in its soil due to intensive overfarming'*.

A handful of soil contains more microorganisms than all the people who have ever lived on earth.

To feed the people we must protect the earth and work with natural systems, rather than seeking to replace them. This is about perma-*culture*.

Voice 2:

Understanding seed, soil and society means celebrating abundance together:

Reader 1:

Psalm 104:10–15 (REB):

You make springs break out in the wadis
so that water from them flows between the hills.
The wild beasts all drink from them.
The wild donkeys quench their thirst.
The birds of the air nest on their banks
and sing among the foliage.
From your dwelling you water the hills.
The earth is enriched by your provision.
You make the grass grow for the cattle
and plants for the use of mortals,
producing grain from the earth,
food to sustain their strength,
wine to gladden the hearts of the people,
and oil to make their faces shine.

Leader:

The people sang this psalm on pilgrimage to the temple. They walked through 'valleys decked with grain' seeing the year crowned with 'good gifts' – filled with wonder and thankfulness not only for food and continuing life but for the sheer beauty of it all.

If you've ever watched the morning light playing on rain-washed apples, looked at sunlit strawberries, red as a trumpet sound, or broad beans and cabbages as green as tomorrow, tasted crusty brown bread, soft at its heart, cheese that crumbles on the tongue and tastes of dew-damp fields, the sweet floweriness of honey or the wonderful harmony of herbs, you'll know that these are magical. And that it's difficult not to sing, dance and be thankful.

That's what abundance is about: not harnessing, enslaving or even storing – but celebrating and sharing.

Sharing is the best food security.

Voice 1:

The psalm is clear about the earth's abundance – it's for sharing.

Hunger in a world of plenty is not caused by lack of food. There is enough food (at the moment) to make most people in the world fat! Hunger is caused by injustice. We don't lack food. We lack compassion: to see how things could be different. Food in all its ordinariness calls us to enter the mystery of our relationship with the earth and our interconnectedness with all life. Our food is sacred; our eating together a holy act, or miracle, not to be taken for granted.

Reader 2: John 6:1–13

Voice 3:

An ordinary miracle

The first to come out of the crowd
as the sun goes down:
a small guardian of the future
with trust in his eyes
and hope in his hands.

In him, Andrew sees something
of himself; meets a memory:
a shadow of long ago when he was a boy,
his energy unsullied and his vision clear;
a whisper from the depths of his being
about fairness and sharing
and simple answers.

A disciple in an impossible position,
reminded of his first care –

to feed others,
wondering about miracles;
a boy bearing food, risking ridicule,
trusting the bread of life:
here, now, late in the day
they make their way
to one whose work
is in such small but costly acts;
who sees in each hungry face
an essential fragility,
a childlike joy
not wholly lost
to a bigger future.

And so ...
in this once-upon-a-time moment ...
the story begins.
Outrageous hope, outspoken love
are released like nudging angels
amongst people longing
for comfort and community,
sensing the beginnings of friendships.

Child, disciple and the one who understands
just and equal sharing:
know there will be enough
to go round;
refuse to say 'It can't be done'.

So it happens – the great feast:
hearts and hands, baskets and pockets,
open;
neighbour gives bread
and peace to neighbour,
each makes a place for another
and in this most ordinary of miracles
all are fed.

Leader:

God of open hands and once-upon-a-time moments,
help us to extend the boundaries of the possible
and continually re-dream the world

Song: 'Hands shaped like a cradle', by Fred Kaan, from *The Only Earth We Know*, Stainer and Bell

Going out:

May food, friendship and thankfulness
nourish our compassion
and give energy to our protest,
so that the time will come
when all share in the feasting
and the fun.

Saints alive!

An all-age service for All Saints'

Nancy Cocks

For the action you will need fish cut-outs with 'Share God's Love' written on them (enough for everyone). This service came from a church named 'Saint John's': churches named for a different saint might adapt the model in order to talk about their saint.

Welcome

Song: 'I sing a song of the saints of God' (various songbooks), or 'The saints of God are down our street', by Ian M. Fraser, *Candles and Conifers*, Wild Goose Publications

Our prayer to greet God:

Holy, holy, holy God, you are greater than we can imagine – invisible like the wind, reliable like a rock, amazing like the stars shining in the night sky. Your love for us is strong and pure. You will never let us go, no matter what happens. And that's why we call you holy, God. You are so good and so pure. Touch us today with your love to make us stronger people. Fill us with your goodness today to make us kinder people so we can follow in the footsteps of Jesus, your holy son and our loving friend. We pray in his name. Amen

Our prayer to say sorry to God:

Holy, holy, holy God, we want to be your people, the friends of Jesus. But sometimes we wonder if we're good enough for you. We make mistakes. We worry about getting our own way. We forget to share your love, and treat other people badly. We are sorry, God. Help us change our ways so your love can shine through our lives.

Leader: Saint John tells us that God is love. And that God's perfect love casts out our fear. (1 John 4:18)

Friends, always remember that when we ask for God to forgive us, God comes to us with perfect love to help us find our way as Jesus' friends.

A conversation about saints: looking for a saint

Children are gathered at the front. Done conversationally:

Do you know what a saint is? …

Any idea about what a saint looks like? …

Who is a saint? …

Where would you look for a saint? …

Pass out hand mirrors.

You are looking at a saint!

A saint is someone who shows us the love of God in action.

Everyone who follows Jesus can look in a mirror and see a saint!

Saints have been around for thousands of years.

Many people we hear about in the Bible are called saints, like Saint John.

Saint John wrote part of the Bible and lived at least 1900 years ago – a long, long time ago.

Saint John teaches us about God by telling us stories about Jesus, and we're going to listen to one of those next. But first, let's sing a song about the stories of Jesus …

Song: 'Tell me the stories of Jesus' (various songbooks)

Now, listen to a story from Saint John, from chapter 6 of his Gospel:

Bible story (John 6:1–14)

Tell the story in an age-appropriate way: use a Children's Bible, etc.

Thinking about the story – saints alive today:

We really can't say how Jesus fed 5000 people with just five loaves and two fish. Five loaves and two fish would make about enough sandwiches for those of us here today! About 100 people, not 5000!

A friend of mine said to me once that maybe when everyone who had a lunch with them that day saw that little boy share his lunch, *they* shared their lunches too. And so there was more than enough to go around. Like a potluck picnic!

We can't really say how things happened that day. But the story makes us wonder what God could make happen if we all shared what we have, in Jesus' name.

Saints share their lives with God's world – just like that boy shared his lunch. And then amazing things happen with God's blessing.

Now, every generation has some saints called John:

John F works in a care home to help older people get up and dressed for the day and live a full life.

John T works in a library to keep it clean and running smoothly and so everyone in our *city/town* can find a good book.

Not every saint is named John of course.

Let me introduce you to some other saints, who share God's love through what they do:

Saint Joan is a nurse.

How does a nurse share God's love in the world? …

Saint Judith is a teacher.

How does a teacher share God's love in the world? …

How do we share God's love together?:

Gather money to help people who are poor or hungry …

Visit people who are lonely or sick or sad …

Make friends with new people …

With a big smile, remind each other that God loves us …

Song: 'I'm gonna live so God can use me' (various songbooks)

Offering

Song of thanksgiving: 'Praise God, from whom all blessings flow' (various songbooks)

Action:

What else can we share in Jesus' name? …

Hand out the fish cut-outs with 'Share God's Love' on them. Let folk sit for a few minutes and think about what else they have to share with others: their family, friends, community, the world … Then encourage folk to talk about this together for a bit.

Folk take the cut-outs home to remind them of what they have to share in Jesus' name.

Prayers for God's people:

Voice 1:   God who loves us all
             and sends us into the world to love each other,
             we thank you today for all those saints
             who have stood by our side,
             holding us in times of joy or sadness,
             listening to us when we needed an ear,
             speaking out for us when we needed a voice.

             In this quiet moment,
             we remember their names with a smile in our hearts …
             Holy God, within us and among us,
All: Help us share ourselves in Jesus' name.

Voice 2:   We thank you today for those saints
who have challenged us to grow, dared us to dream,
inviting us to try new things or follow new paths.

In this quiet moment,
we remember the names of our teachers,
our parents and grandparents
and all those people who have been
a window on the world for us …
Holy God, within us and among us,

All: Help us share ourselves in Jesus' name.

Voice 1:   We thank you today for all those saints
who show us how to love each other,
who touch those in trouble with their time and tenderness,
caring for the sick, cheering the lonely, helping the poor.
In this quiet moment,
we remember the names of people around us
who are in trouble,
and think of those who are sick or lonely,
those who are poor and anyone who needs a helping hand …
Holy God, within us and among us,

All: Help us share ourselves in Jesus' name.

Voice 2:   God of all the saints in every generation,
we would be your saints alive in Jesus' name.
Show us what we have to share with others day by day,
for we give ourselves over to you
in the words of the prayer Jesus taught us:

Lord's Prayer (said together)

Blessing

Song: 'When the saints go marching in' (various songbooks)

March around the church singing this – create a parade of saints!

The saints of God are down our street

A liturgy for All Saints'

Ian M Fraser

Opening

Let us worship God – Father, Son and Holy Spirit. Let us, in wonder, rejoice together at God's creation of humanity.

Reading: Psalm 8

Prayer

Father God, Creator of the wheeling spheres throughout space, we stand in awe before the astounding works of your hands, and in even greater awe before your being, revealed and hidden.

We praise you that you chose us out of all the abounding life you brought into being, asking us to share in the managing of your world, not separating us off from the rest of the world but calling us to be separated off for you in all its ongoing life; and risking giving us free choice to follow or reject your way.

God the Son, of one mind with the Father, who, in the face of our failure to live up to our calling, chose to lay aside the glory of the Godhead to become one with us, sharing our human lot, we marvel at such self-giving love. That, at the last, you, who could have summoned twelve legions of angels to rescue you, drank the cup of humiliation and death, presenting to the Father a humanity which could overcome the world, gives us hope. With such a committed human life before us, we learn to affirm 'God's goodness at the heart of humanity, planted more deeply than all that is wrong'.

God the Holy Spirit, we bless you that the life of Jesus Christ is not given to show up our weakness and failures but to remedy them – to be life-giving for the human race. For you are the one who communicates to us Christ's mind; energises us with his being, offered to indwell ours; bestows forgiveness to restore to us our true selves when we have failed and fallen from grace, affirming us anew as friends and followers. Through you we are called to be saints, made so by grace, confirmed and enlarged in faith through all the ups and downs of life we experience.

Father, Son and Holy Spirit, we adore and bless you who bless us with such a calling and such a heritage. Amen

Hymn: 'The Church's one foundation' (CH4 739)

Old Testament reading: Deuteronomy 7:7–12

Prayer

Lord God, in the face of your greatness the great of this earth have every reason to be humble and the humble have every reason to be lifted high. We bless you for a mother's insight to see in her son a sign that God does not rate people as humans do: 'He has brought down the powerful from their thrones and lifted up the lowly': that no flesh should glory in God's presence, nor in contrast should any human being feel unwanted. Enable us to respond in simplicity of being to whatever may be the character of our own calling, as did Mary: 'Here am I, the servant of the Lord; let it be with me according to your word.'

We bless you that we, in the communion of saints, are a mixed company, helping, through our different gifts, to build up the church, as do different limbs and organs in a body, made one with Jesus Christ, the Head.

Save us from overestimating or underestimating the importance of the part we are to play. We who are all frail are also all precious in your sight, all called to share in your purpose to transform the world in justice, truth and peace.

Enable us, we pray, to be available for whatever may be asked of us. We ask this in Jesus Christ's name. Amen

Hymn: 'Differently gifted' (tune: 'How great Thou art')

Differently gifted, in one band united
as in a body, subject to the Head,
called to be saints, not of their merit chosen
but by your grace and by the Spirit led.

Lord God, not wise, not great in human eyes,
you choose us for your enterprise
to turn the world from evil, hate and sin
and, with us, let salvation in.

Not by themselves do those who journey onwards
strive for a world of justice, truth and peace
but spurred and cheered by those who've gone before them
to fight God's war that earthly wars may cease.

Chorus

Now in our day and this our generation
we're called, as saints, to meet a special claim
and offer back, in years entrusted to us,
a fruitful harvest, worthy of God's name.

Chorus

New Testament reading:

1 Corinthians 1:26–2:5; John 15:16–27

Meditation

We, as saints, are a committed company with work to do. God is the great Doer. We but share in God's doing, taking parts allocated by the Spirit. So if we are to serve God in the world, we must start with worship, giving God the glory, wrestling in prayer, as Jesus did, to find God's will, open to other saints who help us to check on whether we have really read God's mind and not simply used that as a cover for fulfilment of our own desires.

At Pentecost the tongues of fire of the Holy Spirit rested upon everyone present. Whether the life work assigned by the Spirit to each is great or small in the world's eyes, it is entrusted to us for worship and service in the world.

In the New Testament Jesus, the Head of the Body, is presented also as Lord of the world. It was through him that all powers were created and they are meant to serve his purposes. So not only persons but institutions, companies, authorities, marketing powers of different sorts have to be kept under scrutiny by the saints to see that they serve the purposes of God in Christ; and if they are defective, work must be done to get them put right. In the Philippines, Senator Salonga, a Baptist lay preacher, spoke to me of 'the evangelical necessity of research (into multinationals) lest the world get into a powerful grip which is other than God's'.

It is in the calling of the saints to do what is in their power, guided together and strengthened by the Holy Spirit, to see to it that it is God's grip which prevails; and to do this in a differently gifted community of faith and service.

Hymn: 'Rejoice in God's saints, today and all days!' (CH4 742)

Reading: Hebrews 11:32–12:2

Prayer

Lord God, where would we be without those who have gone before? They carved out paths for us to follow.

They endured, as Jesus did, mocking, flaying, torture, death, keeping faith by the power of the Spirit, restored through the gift of forgiveness when they slipped; so that, renewed, they could continue to proclaim and serve.

Among them are those who are specially precious to us. Tell them we love them, we miss them, and long to be with them again once we have given back, over days and years, whatever is looked for in the earthly life entrusted to us.

Glory to the Father, the Son and the Holy Spirit for ever. Amen

Hymn: 'The saints of God are down our street' (Tune: 'The battle hymn of the Republic', CH4 476):

Verses sung by individual voices; the chorus sung by all.

The saints of God are down our street
and round God's throne of light.
There's some with formidable minds
and some just live aright;
together in God's family
their different gifts unite:
God's truth is marching on …

Chorus …

They serve at checkouts, empty bins
and teach and make and mend;
they feed the hungry back from school,
the victimised defend;
to voiceless folk they lend an ear
and immigrants befriend:
God's truth is marching on …

Chorus …

Their efforts gain no accolades,
they just supply that grace
which heals the world of many sores,
renews its battered face,
through such who live and love and care
in their own time and place:
God's truth is marching on …

Chorus …

When death comes knocking at their door
they'll look at Christ askance –
how could such ordinary lives
his Kingdom ends advance?
But Christ will say, 'It's party time –
come, friends, and join the dance!':
God's truth is marching on …

Chorus …

Blessing

A short liturgy of hospitality

John Harvey

Short buzz on experience/knowledge of issues around asylum-seeking/refugees

Music: 'The Refugees', from *Innkeepers and Light Sleepers*, John L. Bell and Graham Maule, Wild Goose Publications

Bible reading: Leviticus 19:33–34

Litany of confession:

If we have known aliens in our community,
and have not loved them as ourselves,
forgive us, God.
FORGIVE US, GOD.

Where we have colluded with unjust laws,
and been insensitive to suffering and fear,
forgive us, God.
FORGIVE US, GOD.

If we have left it to others to offer hospitality
and made excuses to ourselves for inaction,
forgive us, God.
FORGIVE US, GOD.

Where we have remained ignorant of different customs
and assumed that all should observe ours,
forgive us, God.
FORGIVE US, GOD.

God says: 'Do not fear, for I have redeemed you;
I have called you by name, you are mine.'

BEFORE GOD, WITH THE PEOPLE OF GOD,
WE CONFESS TO OUR BROKENNESS:
TO THE WAYS WE WOUND OUR LIVES,
THE LIVES OF OTHERS,
AND THE LIFE OF THE WORLD.

MAY GOD FORGIVE US,
CHRIST RENEW US,
AND THE SPIRIT ENABLE US TO GROW IN LOVE.
AMEN

The Gospel: St Matthew 25:31–40

Litany of hospitality

We pray for all asylum seekers and refugees in this *city/country,*
that they may be able to live among us without fear,
and make their contribution to society in peace.
God, in your mercy,
HEAR OUR PRAYER.

We pray for all civil servants and politicians
who legislate for asylum seekers and refugees,
that they may be moved by humanity and compassion in all they do.
God, in your mercy,
HEAR OUR PRAYER.

We pray for all who write or speak about asylum seekers and refugees
in the media,
that they may be enabled to speak the truth in love.
God, in your mercy,
HEAR OUR PRAYER.

We pray for all victims of racial abuse and violence of any kind,
and for those who perpetrate such acts.
God, in your mercy,
HEAR OUR PRAYER.

We pray for all men and women of goodwill, who seek to offer
true hospitality
to asylum seekers and refugees,
that in so doing they may know
that they offer the hospitality of Christ.

The hospitality of Christ: *sharing bread and wine*

The Peace

The Lord's Prayer

Music: 'The Refugees'

A world full of shelter
A short act of worship

Yvonne Morland

'It is in the shelter of each other that the people live.'
An Irish proverb

Approach

God of many names and many places,
we come to you,
from our lives of privilege,
confident in your promise to shelter us from the storms of life
and from those who persecute us:

'For he will hide me in his shelter in the day of trouble;
he will conceal me under the cover of his tent;
he will set me high upon a rock.' (Psalm 27:5, NRSV)

And yet, we know that even in our own midst
there are people who hunger for peace
and are thirsty for justice in this world …

Hear this and reflect:

Disputed world

Sukkot in Jerusalem,
families build shelters
for the Feast of Tabernacles;
an honoured remembering
of exiled ancestors,
fragile in the desert
after escape from Egypt.
Across disputed ground,
exiles in their own land
live with no shelter,
homes now rubble,
and no security;

a fragile desert,
with no escape.

How can this be
if we are under one God,
in the shelter of God's wings?
Yet man, not God,
has pulled the feathers off,
in mindless acts of violence,
leaving us all exposed
to the winds of war.

Prayer

We bring to you anew, our God,
the hundreds of refugees who are fleeing
conflict and persecution in their own lands
often to be met by hostility and meanness of spirit.

*'They are wet with the rain of the mountains,
and cling to the rock for want of shelter.'* (Job 24:8)

Bring to our hearts a deep understanding
that it is our task to reach out in friendship
to those who are so sorely pressed
and, in your name, give comfort and hope.

Give us courage to be

*'... a refuge to the poor,
a refuge to the needy in their distress,
a shelter from the rainstorm
and a shade from the heat.'* (Isaiah 25:4)

Hear this and reflect:

Our world

In my world
I have shelter,
food and friends,
a place where I belong,
in a country I love
and in which I live.

In your world
any shelter you have
is temporary, stigmatised;
you are dependent on others
for food and friendship,
your country lost to you.

We live in the same world,
yet we do not;
we have the same needs,
for love, warmth and friends,
yet your needs are not
recognised by all.

I cannot begin to show
the kind of courage
you have shown

in an open boat on a hostile sea,
in walking miles across borders,
in seeing children starve or drown,
in hoping and believing
in a better life ahead.

My world is diminished
by the suffering in yours,
but self-pity
is no tribute to you,
brother and sister in my heart,
child of my human frailty.

You are welcome in our world.

We are told:

'It is in the shelter of each other that the people live.'

And we know that *'God has no other hands than ours'* (St Teresa of Ávila).

We ask you to bless us, God,
and all those who suffer and are persecuted,
so that together
we may build a world full of shelter that will
withstand the storms of life
and offer freedom and sanctuary.
Amen

Song: 'Do not be afraid' (various songbooks)

Swords into ploughshares
A short liturgy

John Harvey

Reading: We Shall Overcome

'I have the audacity to believe that peoples everywhere can have three meals a day for their bodies, education and culture for their minds, and dignity, equality and freedom for their spirits. I believe that what self-centred men have torn down men other-centred can build up. I still believe that one day mankind will bow before the altars of God and be crowned triumphant over war and bloodshed, and nonviolent redemptive good will proclaim the rule of the land. "And the lion and the lamb shall lie down together and every man shall sit under his own vine and fig tree and none shall be afraid." I still believe that We Shall overcome! ...'

Martin Luther King Jr, from his Nobel Peace Prize acceptance speech, 1964 (Taken from Nobel Prize.org, the Nobel Foundation website. Copyright © The Nobel Foundation 1964)

Song: 'Jesus Christ is waiting' (*Heaven Shall Not Wait*, John L. Bell and Graham Maule, Wild Goose Publications)

Prayer of confession

For our incapacity to feel the sufferings of others,
and our tendency to live comfortably with injustice,
GOD FORGIVE US.

For the self-righteousness which denies guilt,
and the self-interest which strangles compassion,
GOD FORGIVE US.

For those who live their lives in careless unconcern,
who cry 'Peace, peace' when there is no peace,
WE ASK YOUR MERCY.

For our failings in community,
our lack of understanding,
WE ASK YOUR MERCY.

For our lack of forgiveness, openness, sensitivity,
GOD FORGIVE US.

For the times we were too eager to be better than others,
when we are too rushed to care,
when we are too tired to bother,
when we don't really listen,
when we are too quick to act from motives other than love,
GOD FORGIVE US.

Silence

Bible reading

Stories

Closing prayer

Jesus invites us to a way of celebration,
meeting and feasting with the humble and poor.
LET US WALK HIS WAY WITH JOY.

Jesus beckons us to a way of risk,
letting go of our security.
LET US WALK HIS WAY WITH JOY.

Jesus challenges us to listen to the voices
of those who have nothing to lose.
LET US WALK HIS WAY WITH JOY.

Jesus points us to a way of self-giving,
where power and status are overturned.
LET US WALK HIS WAY WITH JOY.

Jesus calls us to follow the way of the cross,
where despair is transformed by the promise of new life.
LET US WALK HIS WAY WITH JOY.

The Grace

May the grace of the Lord Jesus Christ
and the love of God
and the fellowship of the Holy Spirit
be with us all
Amen

Now come two hearts
A blessing liturgy for a marriage
or partnership

Thom M Shuman

Processional

Opening words

We have come to this sacred space,
for God is here:
    the One who guided the stars
    into their places in the night sky
has brought us here to witness
the bouquet of joyous wonder
which the seeds of love have brought forth.

We have come together in this holy moment,
for Jesus is here:
    the One who fills our hearts
    to the brim with hope
has brought us here to see them emptied
in words and acts of self-giving love.

We have come for this joy,
for the Spirit is here:
    for the One who washes us
    in the gentle waters of grace
has brought us here to be bathed
in the gentle light shining in lovers' eyes.

Now, we have come,
God in Community, Holy and One,
    for you have brought us to celebrate
    your gift of eternal love
made human in *(name)* and *(name)*.

Declaration of intent

In a moment of exquisite wonder, you were created to be one with God;
in the waters of baptism, you were named beloved,
    so you might be one with Jesus;

in the warmth of your passion, you were filled with grace,
    so you might be one with the Spirit.

(Bride), do you wish to become one with *(groom)*? To be his healing balm in moments of anguish; to be his friend when others turn away; to be the mirror of his soul, so he might see God's love, God's hope, God's delight in him?

Bride: I do.

(Groom), do you wish to become one with *(bride)*? To be her healing balm in moments of anguish; to be her friend when others turn away; to be the mirror of her soul, so she might see God's love, God's hope, God's delight in her?

Groom: I do.

Affirmation of the families

When *(name)* and *(name)* took their first breath, you were there;
when they faltered on that first step, you were there;
when they spoke their first words, you were there;
whenever and wherever, as parents, as siblings, as relatives,
you have journeyed with them.

So now, as *(name)* and *(name)* whisper their love to one another,
as they take their first steps as partners in life,
as they use words to describe the fullness of their hearts,
I ask you to surround them with your love, your hopes, your joy.

DEAR ONES, OUR TEARS ARE THOSE OF JOY.
OUR HEARTS MELT IN THE WARMTH OF YOUR LOVE.
OUR PRAYERS, OUR SUPPORT, OUR HOPES
ARE THE GIFTS WE OFFER TO YOU IN THIS MOMENT
AND IN ALL THE MOMENTS TO COME.

Prayer

Now come two hearts
    to beat as one;
may the grace of your love
    unite them, Heartsong.

Now come two lives
    to serve as one;
may the justice of your love
    make them one, Servant of the poor.

Now come two souls
    to live as one;
may the peace of your love
    guide them, Tender Spirit.

Now, God in Community, Holy and One,
    pour yourself into *(name)* and *(name)*.
In this moment of exquisite joy
    and in all the moments to come. Amen

Readings

Homily

Hymn

Speaking promises to each other

As God loves unconditionally, so I love you;
as Jesus became servant of the poor, so I will serve you;
as the Spirit comforts, so I will cradle you in my heart;
    as light is to the eye,
    as joy is to the heart,

may your spirit be with me,
(bride's name) of my heart,
until time is no more.

As God loves unconditionally, so I love you;
as Jesus became servant of the poor, so I will serve you;
as the Spirit comforts, so I will cradle you in my heart;
as light is to the eye,
as joy is to the heart,
may your spirit be with me,
(groom's name) of my heart,
until time is no more.

Exchanging of the rings

Blessing of the rings

Giving of the rings *(to be repeated after the minister)*

As a circle has no end,
I surround you with my wonder;
on our journey which is just beginning,
I will walk hand in hand each day with you;
as a sunrise heralds a new day,
I will see you with new joy in each moment;
as God gives us the sign of never-ending love in Jesus,
I grace you with this ring
as a sign and seal of my life with you,

in the name of the Father
and of the Son,
and of the Holy Spirit,
God in Community, Holy and One. Amen

Announcement of marriage

Concluding prayer

If it was only our love which brings us together,
we might wonder how long we could endure.
But it is your love, Imaginative God,
that is the foundation of any love we might feel or share.
    That love which cradled the moon and sun
        in the sky above
    is the love that opens our eyes
        to the joy shining in our beloved's;
    that love which caused the rivers to flow
        through lush valleys
    is the love that can spring forth, fresh and clear,
        in the deserts of our souls.
May that love be the bedrock of *(names)* marriage.

If it was only chance which brings us together,
we might doubt the words spoken, the promises made.
But it is your grace, Jesus of our hearts,
which is mortar that seals lovers together.
    That grace which saw God
        in every person you met,
    is the grace that opens our hearts
        to embrace the gift of the other;
    that grace which dared to reach out, without reservation,
        to bring healing and hope to the broken,
    is the grace that enables us to risk giving ourselves
        completely to another.
May that grace be the bond which binds
    (name) and *(name)* from this time on.

If it was only passion which brings us together,
we might question when it will dissipate.
But it is your peace, Spirit of Delight,
which is the fire that warms us on the cool days.
    That peace which tiptoed
        in the dew of Eden's dawn,
    is the peace that teaches us
        new steps, new songs, new hopes.

That peace which lullabies the wind to sleep
    on stormy nights,
is the peace that gifts us with the silence
    to cradle our lover's deepest longings.
May that peace be the eternal flame forever warming
    (name) and *(name)*.

If it was only us, we might wonder what the days
ahead might bring, God in Community, Holy and One,
but with you in the silence and the songs,
    in the wonder and the words,
    in the delight and the dancing,
(name) and *(name)* can begin their journey.
Your love, your grace, your peace upon them. Amen.

Benediction

May the peace of the rolling waves,
the peace of the silent mountains,
the peace of the singing stars,
and the deep, deep peace of the Prince of Peace
be with you now, and for ever. Amen

The blessed path
A wedding/partnership ceremony

Annie Heppenstall

Planning guidance

Below are some questions and thoughts to reflect on during the preparation process.

Thinking 'big picture', what has been the journey that brought you to this point? What is it that has drawn you together so strongly? Who and what are your shared loves? What are your shared visions and hopes? How might you reflect this unique story of your relationship in the ceremony?

As you bring ideas together, it's worth thinking about three essential elements:

- *visual* (colours, clothes, flowers, other decorations such as fabrics and candles, meaningful symbols); .
- *audio* (live music & musicians, recordings, readings, poetry, hymns or other songs or chants ...);
- *space and movement* (timing, smoothness, moving from one position to another, rituals such as rings and hand-fasting, use of physical space, furniture, people).

Who is coming to take part in the ceremony, and what room are you using? How do you want your guests to be seated? In rows, the two families on either side of an aisle? In a semicircle, all mixed together? What options are possible in the venue you have chosen? Are there parents and/or step-parents who will play a role, or children from a previous partnership? Who will officiate? Do you want them or somebody else to give an address?

How do you want to begin the ceremony? Do you want to do it the traditional way, with the bride on the arm of the father and the groom waiting at the altar? The symbolism of this is 'giving away': the transfer from the childhood home to the marital home. Is this what you want to represent? What about walking up with a different significant and supportive person or people? Or what about walking in together as a couple? (This may appeal to you particularly if you left the childhood home quite a while ago!)

Do you have the support of a choir (formal or informal), who can lead singing? If not, you might prefer to choose simpler or more familiar hymns.

The focal point of the ceremony is the exchange of vows and the pronouncement. How do you want to draw special attention to this? Will you both have rings? Will they be brought up on a cushion or in a box for the minister to bless? Will they be waiting on the altar? What do the rings mean to you?

When you have made your vows, would you like your hands to be joined only for a few moments, during the blessing, or would you like more emphasis on hand-fasting? Would you like to raise your joined hands for all to see? Do you want the minister's stole wrapped around your hands, or do you want to use a special ribbon that will be waiting on the altar?

At the end, are you two going to walk out first, and invite everyone to follow? Once the ceremony is over, how can you make sure you have a few minutes of privacy together, before the celebrations start?

With the minister/leader of your ceremony, consider which of the different options in the ceremony are to be used, including how you are to be referred to (husband & wife, partners for life, etc) and how the suggested service will really come alive for your own unique occasion.

Hymns

Here are some suggested hymns. Most of the melodies are easy to pick up.

- *All are welcome/Let us build a house where love can dwell:* Marty Haugen
- *Amen siyakudumisa* (Amen! Praise the name of the Lord!): South African traditional
- *As two we love are wed this day:* John L Bell
- *Brother, sister, let me serve you, let me be as Christ to you:* Richard Gillard
- *God to enfold you, Christ to uphold you:* John L Bell
- *How good it is, what pleasure comes, when people live as one:* Ruth Duck
- *Love is the touch of intangible joy:* Alison Robertson & John L Bell
- *Oh the life of the world is a joy and a treasure:* Kathy Galloway, Ian Galloway & John L Bell
- *One more step along the world I go:* Sydney Carter
- *Peruvian Gloria:* Liturgical text, traditional Peruvian, with leader & response
- *Put peace into each other's hands:* John L Bell
- *Sing of the Lord's goodness, Father of all wisdom:* Ernest Sands

- *Sing to God with gladness, all creation:* James Quinn & John L Bell
- *There's a spirit in the air:* Brian Wren & John Wilson
- *You shall go out with joy and be led forth with peace:* Stuart Dauermann

In the service below, reference is made to the Taizé chant *Ubi Caritas* (Where there is love there is God). Taizé chants are popular, simple and easy to get hold of; there are many others which might appeal to you, such as:

- *The Lord is my light, my light and salvation*
- *Laudate Dominum* (based on Psalm 117, the call for all people to praise God)
- *Bless the Lord, my soul*

Readings

You may have significant poems, letters and other texts that you want to include. Some suggestions for readings from the Bible follow:

Relationships with loving qualities
- Isaac and Rebekah: Gen 24:58-67
- Ruth and Naomi: Ruth 1:16-18
- Jonathan and David: 1 Samuel 17:58-18:5

Love
- 1 Corinthians 13
- Song of Songs (read all of it and pick your favourite passage!) – NB the ceremony below makes some use of passages from the Song of Songs.
- 1 John 4:7-11

Marriage
- Isaiah 61:10-11
- Wedding at Cana: John 2:1-11
- (Of the lamb) Revelation 19:5-10

Joy over God's blessings
- Psalm 36:5-10

- Psalm 67
- Psalm 121

Journeying under God's care/in God's presence
- The glory-cloud of God's presence: Exodus 40:34-38
- Psalm 23
- You shall go out with joy: Isaiah 55:8-13
- Where can I go from your spirit?: Psalm 139:1-18, 23-24

The ceremony

Introduction

Gathering of the community to witness commitment and show support for the couple

Opening hymn/music of choice for the entrance of the procession

Leader (addressing the congregation):

We are here to witness the marriage [blessing of partnership] between N___ and N___, in the presence of God, who is love.

Today, we stand at a special place, on holy ground. We stand at a meeting place where two paths draw together and become one path, stretching into the future. You have gathered here because in your own ways you have walked with N___ and N___; so now please join in blessing these two travellers of the way.

Community to couple:

N___ and N___ of our love,
N___ and N___ of God's bounteous love,
together may you find
God behind you, God above you,
God within you and around you,
shielding you from any harm,
guiding every step you take
on this the blessed path you tread.
Amen

Invocation/prayer addressing couple:

Leader:

N___ and N___, may you be blessed today and every day,
with all the blessings of God's abundant grace,
and may God be with you in every valley,
Jesus be with you on every hill,
Spirit be with you on every road,
headland, ridge and city street.
Each sea and land, each moor and meadow,
each lying down, each rising up,
each step of the journey you take,
may you be blessed!
All: **Amen**

(adapted from *Carmina Gadelica* 275 The Pilgrim's Aiding)

Hymn/song of choice

'The Word'

Optional leader's introduction to the readings:

As we travel through the joys and challenges of life, we find inspiration in the qualities of others who have loved deeply.

In the Bible, we find many expressions of that deep love. The Song of Songs celebrates the equal and passionate delight that lovers find in one another.

The book of Ruth describes the strength of devotion Ruth has for Naomi; we are touched by the gift of loving service for the good of the other.

In the accounts of the Kings we hear of David and Jonathan, whose loving loyalty to one another surpassed all, even fear of death and loss of status.

In the book of Genesis, we read of Rebekah and Isaac, who found comfort in one another's embrace, and strength to face a long life together.

We find inspiration, too, in the message of joy and hope, of God's abundant goodness and rich blessings on all the earth, for which we give thanks today.

But we find inspiration especially in the many affirmations of God's presence with us no matter what; for God's love for us is a greater loyalty even than that of Jonathan, a greater act of service than that of Ruth, a greater comfort even than the arms of Rebekah. This is the gift by which N___ and N___ are blessed as they walk together in God's love.

A reading / readings
(see list of suggestions above)

Option: separate readings with a short repeated song such as the Taizé chant Ubi Caritas *(Where there is love there is God) or* Amen siyakudumisa *(see list of hymns above)*

A Psalm/canticle: leader and response
(choice of two)

EITHER:

Song of Songs 2:10–13

Leader:

My beloved speaks and says to me:
'Arise, my love, my fair one, and come away;

All:

for now the winter is past, the rain is over and gone.

The flowers appear on the earth; the time of singing has come, and the voice of the turtledove is heard in our land.

The fig tree puts forth its figs, and the vines are in blossom; they give forth fragrance.

Arise, my love, my fair one, and come away;

for now the winter is past, the rain is over and gone.
The flowers appear on the earth; the time of singing has come.'

OR:

Psalm 85:8–12

Leader:

Let me hear what God the Lord will speak,
for he will speak peace to his people,
to his faithful, to those who turn to him in their hearts.

All:

Surely his salvation is at hand for those who fear him,
that his glory may dwell in our land.

Steadfast love and faithfulness will meet;
righteousness and peace will kiss each other.

Faithfulness will spring up from the ground,
and righteousness will look down from the sky.

The Lord will give what is good,
and our land will yield its increase.

Steadfast love and faithfulness will meet;
righteousness and peace will kiss each other.

Option: short address by leader/other

Hymn

Declarations of commitment

by couple, gathered community / interested parties, e.g. children

Leader:

Now, we have declarations to make in the presence of one another and God.

(to the gathered community)

Are you here with love in your hearts, for the sake of sharing N___ and N___'s joy?

All:

Yes, we are.

Will you continue to love N___ and N___, supporting and affirming their love for one another, in the years that come?

We will.

(Optional, to any significant participants such as parents or children)

Will you play your part in helping N and N always to strengthen and deepen their love?

We / I will.

(To each of the couple, in turn)

Do you, N___, love N___ with all your heart,
desiring no other;
and do you truly want to walk with N___,
on rough ground and on smooth,
whether the way is easy
or whether it demands all the courage and strength that you have?

I do.

(To both)

And do you seek together,
God's presence as your shepherd,
guiding you both and loving you both
as you make your way hand in hand,
living in hope that though death part you,
in God, your love can never die?

We do.

Couple, in turn, to one another:

N___, set me as a seal upon your heart,
as a seal upon your arm;
for love is strong as death,
passion fierce as the grave.
Its flashes are flashes of fire,
a raging flame.

All (waiting until both have spoken):

Many waters cannot quench love,
neither can floods drown it.
If one offered for love
all the wealth of one's house,
it would be utterly scorned.

(Song of Songs 8:6–7)

Marriage vows

EITHER:

Leader, turning to each of the couple in turn to repeat the same promises:

N___, do you take N___ as your [lawful spouse/wife/husband/partner]
to cherish and love,
to honour and respect,
to stand by and travel with,
wherever the way may lead
and whatever may lie ahead?
I do.

And do you vow before God and your gathered community
that you will share gladly with N___ all that you are and all that you have,
and, with delight, welcome all that N___ is and all N___ gives?

I do.

OR:

Leader gives lines for each to repeat:

I, N___, take you, N___, as my [......]
to cherish and love,
to honour and respect,
to stand by and travel with
wherever the way may lead
and whatever may lie ahead.

And I vow before God and our gathered community,
that I will share gladly with you
all that I am and all that I have,
and, with delight, welcome all that you are
and all that you give.

Exchange of rings and pronouncement

Leader:

N___ and N___ will now give each other rings, as a sign of the commitment they have made and the binding nature of their love.

Ring blessing

Leader prays, holding a hand of blessing over the rings:

May these rings serve as a constant and joyful reminder of what God has said:

'I have loved you with an everlasting love;
therefore I have continued my faithfulness to you.'

(Jeremiah 31:3)

So may these rings be a sign of the love and faithfulness between N___ and N___.

All:

Amen

In turn, each takes the other's hand and places a ring on the ring finger, saying,

N___, wear this ring and remember always that my love for you is deep and wide and grows ever greater.

The couple join hands and the leader wraps his / her stole around their hands, or a specially prepared ribbon.

Leader:

God is witness to this union. Where two have become one in love, let no one seek to break this sacred bond.

Blessing

All:

The blessing of the Most High be yours,
and well may it keep you;

Christ's blessing be yours,
and encircle you with love;

Holy Spirit's blessing be yours,
and gladly may you spend your lives,

each day that you rise up,
each night that you lie down.

So may God, who is Love,
aid you and shepherd you at all times,
and pour rich and generous blessings upon you.
Amen

(adapted from *Carmina Gadelica* 277 misc. blessings)

Leader:

I now pronounce N___ and N___ [husband and wife/loving partners for life …]

Hands are untied, ribbon may be placed on altar

Song / music
(register signing can take place now if required)

Concluding prayers

Leader:

All our thanks and praise are to you, eternal God,
for blessing humanity
with the gift of profound and intimate love.

All:

Thanks and praise to you, Eternal One

Especially today we give thanks
that you brought N___ and N___ together,
and sowed in them the desire
to give themselves, one to the other.

Thanks and praise to you, O Christ

Let the love that has grown between N___ and N___
flourish and bear rich fruit,
that all who know them
may be touched by grace, by joy and the deep peace
that only you can give.

Thanks and praise to you, O Holy Spirit

So may N___ and N___ go out from here
confident in your blessings upon them,
strong in your Spirit and joyful in their hearts,
ready to step out onto the path that lies ahead,
travellers together on the Way.

Thanks and praise to you, O God.
Amen

Leader reads Ephesians 3:14–19 as a closing blessing for the couple.

Closing hymn/music of choice

Eucharist liturgy can follow here if desired, or couple lead out, followed by congregation, for celebration.

An invocation
and celebration of love

Annie Heppenstall

Preparation notes

This liturgy requires one or more people to act as leaders and readers and all others to join in with the shared responses and singing. The reader of the reflection needs to be chosen with some care and if possible given the text in advance, due to the length of the passage.

Bear in mind special considerations to help all participate as fully as possible. Is the table accessible? Are all speakers audible? Would large print options help? Are there tactile / other sensory elements?

Arrange seating in a circle with a low table in the centre. Place flowers or potted plants on the table and sufficient tea lights or small candles for all present to light at least one, with suitable fire precautions.

Choose appropriate music to play softly before and at points during the liturgy. Consider the theme, the intended mood and likely participants. Classical music? Choral music? Folk? Contemporary? Do you have musicians who might play?

In the same vein, consider what songs / chants are suitable based on the suggestions in the liturgy and whether you will need recordings or musicians / a singer who can lead.

Decide how long to hold the silence for. Most people, including children, can manage a minute or two if given a focus; anything between this and ten or fifteen minutes might be appropriate depending on the group, but it helps to tell people how long they have. You might like to begin and end the silence by ringing a meditation bell.

Consider inviting people in advance to bring pictures or objects representing loved ones or loved things, places, creatures, etc. they would like to celebrate, which they can place on the central table to be 'present' during the liturgy. Also add natural objects or flowers and pieces of paper and pens for people who have come unprepared.

It may feel appropriate to invite people to say a little about the loves they are bringing, followed by a brief silence before continuing the liturgy. Or this could take place at the end. It could lead into a longer activity, such as a creative session making something to express love, gratitude for love, memory of love using dance, modelling, paints, textiles, natural objects … Planning for this will depend on resources, age of participants and time.

The biblical quotations are from the NRSV translation.

The liturgy

Music

Opening

Leader: Welcome to our celebration of love!
Beloved, let us love one another, because love is from God;

All: **everyone who loves is born of God and knows God.**

Leader: Whoever does not love does not know God, for God is love.

All: **If we love one another, God lives in us, and God's love is perfected in us.**

1 John 4:7–8,12

Leader: Mother-Father God, by your infinite love,
all is conceived and brought to birth,
all life animated by your breath,
all souls embraced by the outstretched arms
of your son, our brother.

All: **We join together today,
lovers of life, lovers of Christ,
lovers of your great mystery,
living and dying and embracing new life,
ever closer to our home in your own perfect love.
Amen[1]**

Dedicating

Leader: Let us dedicate this time to invoking love and to giving thanks
for love, for people, creatures, places, memories that we love,
and for those who love us.

While the music plays, you are invited to place names, pictures
or other tokens representing your loves on the table in the
centre.

There are pens, paper and natural objects if you want to use
them.

Music, while tokens of love are brought to the table.

Fade music out.

[Optional time to talk about what has been placed on table]

Pause

Leader: Let us give thanks for these tokens of love:

All: **All things come from you, O God, and of your own do we
give you.**

Seeking God's love

Leader: The psalms help us speak of love for God:

O God, you are my God, I seek you,
my soul thirsts for you;
my flesh faints for you,
as in a dry and weary land where there is no water.

All: **So I have looked upon you in the sanctuary,
beholding your power and glory.
Because your steadfast love is better than life,
my lips will praise you.**

Leader: So I will bless you as long as I live;
            I will lift up my hands and call on your name.
            My soul is satisfied as with a rich feast,
            and my mouth praises you with joyful lips

All: **when I think of you on my bed,**
            and meditate on you in the watches of the night;
            for you have been my help,
            and in the shadow of your wings I sing for joy.

            Psalm 63:1–7

*Sing together 'In love you summon', John Bell (There is One Among Us, Wild
Goose Publications) or similarly simple alternative on the theme of love.*

Pause

Leader: The Song of Songs is rich in the language of love, taken by
            mystics to represent the soul's longing for God ...

            Upon my bed at night
            I sought him whom my soul loves;

All: **I sought him, but found him not;**
            I called him, but he gave no answer.

Leader: 'I will rise now and go about the city,
            in the streets and in the squares;

All: **I will seek him whom my soul loves.'**
            Song of Songs 3:1–2

All: **God our soul's magnet,**
            may we be drawn to you,
            fall in love with you,
            follow you with a lover's devotion
            to the humanity and the divinity
            at the heart of the city.[2]
            Amen

Repeat the song used above

Pause

First reader:

Show me where I can open
unconstrained
to you, great Love,
pour out my heart
then let you pour yourself
into the space that I have made
like liquid gold,
a well of living water
bubbling up within.[3]
Amen

Reflection

Leader / second reader:

A reflection from the introduction to *The Healer's Tree* by Annie Heppenstall

'Arise my love, my fair one,
and come away ...
the time of singing has come.'

Song of Songs 2:10,12

The Song of Songs describes a lover standing at the latticed window of a house, calling to their beloved to come outside and share the delights of a beautiful garden. It is a love poem, a form that mystics throughout the ages have used to speak of the soul's relationship with God. That call, 'Arise my love, my fair one,' is addressed to each of us, and the 'singing time' is now.

The Song of Songs continues, '... the voice of the turtle dove is heard in our land. The fig tree puts forth its figs, and the vines are in blossom ...' (S of S 2:12-13). That special song is the natural chorus of creation, life itself, in which we have our own part. It is the definitive love song that enlivens us as we grow in the womb, that sits on the tip of our tongue throughout our lives, and serenades us as we pass through the veil of death. It is a song that never ends. But, like someone who has fallen asleep, we sometimes need waking to it, because we easily forget that we belong not only to God, but also to the earth and to the whole matrix of life.

This living song is the narrative of the great human adventure mapped out in the Bible. Like Adam and Eve, we begin as loved creatures full of God's goodness. We fall, we suffer, we strive, but God is still with us in our wandering, and defeats death itself to bring us back into the divine embrace, restored to the 'all in all'.

When we hear the call, respond, and step out of our enclosures and from behind our walls into the garden, even for a second, life looks different. Motives change, inner healing begins, acts of love spring up from us like rings of toadstools on an autumn lawn. We are new creations.

But crucially, opening to God is a path of joy and peace not just for ourselves, but for all the earth. In God, we can no longer act only for ourselves and our own salvation. 'Self' loses its power and the illusion of isolation ends, for all creation is interconnected. The kingdom of God is built on selflessness not selfishness. It is not just we who are renewed; all creation depends on our return for its renewal.

It is this deep healing that the earth cries out for today, and our hearts too. It is as though the destruction of the earth mirrors our inner desolation, which arises from the separation we feel from that glorious primal garden. Restoration of right relationship with God means restoration also of relationship with God's creation – we can no longer see ourselves in isolation. We have some work to do to bring that about, both in the outer world and in the inner world of our hearts, but what we seek, Jesus says, we will find, and when we knock, doors will open.[4]

Pause with short silence or music to listen to.

Leader: My beloved speaks and says to me:
      'Arise, my love, my fair one,
      and come away;

All: **for now the winter is past,**
the rain is over and gone.

Leader: The flowers appear on the earth;
the time of singing has come,

All: **and the voice of the turtle dove**
is heard in our land.

Leader: The fig tree puts forth its figs,
and the vines are in blossom;
they give forth fragrance.

All: **Arise, my love, my fair one,**
and come away.

Loving God,
let me come away with you
to that place of gladness, that time of singing,
to know the truth of your most precious love,
for the satisfaction of my deepest need.
And through my own discovery of delight in you,
may I become as one who can bring others
to your healing love,
for by sharing this love, it can only grow.
Amen[5]

Just 'being' in love

Leader: As Paul wrote to the people of Rome:

'I am convinced that neither death, nor life, nor angels, nor
rulers, nor things present, nor things to come, nor powers, nor
height, nor depth, nor anything else in all creation, will be able
to separate us from the love of God in Christ Jesus our Lord.'

Romans 8:38–39 NRSV

So let us sit for a while in the knowledge and hope of that divine
love, all around and deep within, blessing the whole of creation.
Let us breathe deep of that love and let it touch us, heart and soul.

We will hold the silence for [4] minutes.

Active participation

Leader: Now, in the quiet, we bring to mind the gift, the quality of love itself.

All: **For love, which is God, we give thanks.**

Leader: Let us light candles to express the love in our own hearts, brought out to share with the world.

Candles on the central table are lit.

Sing Taizé chant 'Ubi Caritas'* during candle-lighting and continue for a while after all have participated.

(*The chant means 'Where there is charity and love, there is God')

Pause in silence

[Optional time to talk about what has been placed on table]

Closing prayer

All: **God of our brother Jesus,**
            your love is the love of a mother
            who adores her children and forgives them everything.
            Your love is the love of a father
            who is devoted to his children and accepts them always.
            We are your children.
            We fall down and you help us up.
            We go wrong and you put us right.
            Now, fill our emptiness with your love,
            replace our brokenness with wholeness,
            and our weakness with your strength,
            that we might go out into the world and be of use to you.
            Amen[6]

Sources:

1   Adapted from *Wild Goose Chase*, Annie Heppenstall, Wild Goose Publications 2006, p.213

2   From *Wild Goose Chase*, Annie Heppenstall, Wild Goose Publications 2006, p.190

3   From *The Healer's Tree*, Annie Heppenstall, Wild Goose Publications 2011, p.107

4   From *The Healer's Tree*, Annie Heppenstall, Wild Goose Publications 2011, p.9-10

5   From *Wild Goose Chase*, Annie Heppenstall, Wild Goose Publications 2006, p.69

6   From *Wild Goose Chase*, Annie Heppenstall, Wild Goose Publications 2006, p.211

Friends of the Lord

An all-age service about friendship

Nancy Cocks

Introduction:

In this approach to all-age worship an adult leads the service and conversational times with the children, who gather close to the front of the church. Other parts can be taken by children and youth.

In preparation have the children/youth group make friendship bracelets (enough for everyone in the congregation).

Opening words:

Listen to important words from Jesus:

No one has greater love than this: to lay down one's life for one's friend. You are my friends if you do what I ask you … And this is what I ask you: that you love one another as I have loved you. (John 15)

Song: 'Amigos de Cristo' (traditional Latin American song)

Prayers:

We say good morning to God:

Good morning, God! We are here as your family to sing your praise today. We are here as friends of Jesus to share your love with each other today and every day. We are glad for your gift of love which touches our lives in so many ways. Today, help us think about the ways we can touch other lives we love, because we are friends of the Lord!

We say sorry to God:

Dear God, as we sit here quietly, we can think of times we didn't act like a very good friend. Sometimes we haven't kept our promises. Sometimes we've talked about others behind their back. Sometimes we've been angry with a friend and never worked things out. We're sorry, God, that we don't always act like friends of the Lord.

We hear a kind word about God:

Dear friends, while it is true we have all done things we shouldn't have and disappointed God, it is also true that God forgives us when we own up to what we've done. With Jesus' love we can become new people. So know that we make God glad when we remember to say we're sorry. We can show Jesus' love by saying sorry to our friends – and that will make God glad too!

Talking about what matters: what makes a good friend?:

- *How does a good friend treat you? ...*

- *How do you feel when you know you have a good friend? A best friend? ...*

- *Jesus calls us his friends, and says if we are his friends, then we should love each other ...*

- *How can we show Jesus' love to our friends? ...*

Our story today helps us think about what can sometimes happen between friends to test a friendship:

Fergie's best friend:

Narrator: One day Fergie the frog was very excited when he hopped home from school.

Mother Frog: 'What's new?' asked Mother Frog, as she peeled the cattails for stew.

Fergie: 'I made a new friend today – he's fantastic. He's the biggest frog in our class. He tells great jokes. He's the best swimmer. And he gave me one of his toad-jam tarts at lunch.'

Mother Frog: 'Sounds like quite a frog! What's his name?'

Fergie: 'Bill Frog. But I get to call him Bull. That's his nickname.'

Narrator: Fergie did everything with his new friend Bull. They sailed lily pads in the swamp. They explored the creek. They ate mosquito-ripple ice cream. One day Fergie's mother said,

Mother Frog: 'Roger called to see you this afternoon.'

Fergie: 'Roger? Oh, Roger. What did he want? He knew Bull and I were practising our dives at the old rock.'

Mother Frog: 'I thought Roger was your best friend.'

Fergie: 'Nope. Not any more. It's Bull and Fergie now. Fergie and Bull – we're a team. He's the greatest. Mum, he told the funniest story at lunch today about a caterpillar and a crocodile ...'

Narrator: In Fergie's eyes, Bull Frog could do no wrong. He was the best frog in the whole swamp. Fergie did everything with Bull – until the day that Bull met a girl frog. Then Fergie came home early for supper.

Mother Frog: 'Where's Bull? Isn't he coming for supper? I made extra macaroni and fleas.'

Fergie: 'He's not coming. He went to Felicity Frog's place – again. That's the fourth time this week. I don't think Bull and I are going to be friends any more.'

Mother Frog: 'Then why don't you call Roger? He might come for supper and stay over tonight.'

Fergie: 'Good idea!'

Narrator: But then Fergie gulped,

Fergie: 'I hope Roger will still be my friend.'

Narrator: Sure enough, Roger came over for supper that night. The two old friends played hide-and-seek until the moon rose. Then, as the two frogs snuggled into the mud, Fergie said:

Fergie: 'Thanks for coming over tonight. Sorry I was so dumb to waste my time with Bull Frog lately. Still friends?'

Narrator: 'Sure,' said Roger. 'I always knew you were dumb, Fergie. That's why you're my best friend.' Roger smiled as Fergie poked him. 'Same old Fergie,' said Roger.

Fergie: 'Same old Roger!'

Narrator: And the two best friends sank into the mud and went to sleep.

Talking about the story together:

When a friend stops being a friend, it hurts deep down inside.

It can feel terrible if your best friend finds a new best friend.

What makes you wonder if one of your friends isn't a friend any more? ...

(Things children said in the service:

– They walk right past you as if you weren't there.

– They say mean things about you behind your back, or to your face.

– They 'forget' to come over when you planned to do something together.

– No Valentine! ...)

Best friends are friends who will be there for us whenever we need them – like Roger was for Fergie! – even after we've let them down.

That's the kind of friend Jesus is: one who takes us back even after we've let him down.

And that's the kind of friend we can be for someone else – with Jesus' love inside us.

A 'repeat after me' prayer:

(Done line by line: leader then congregation)

Jesus,
thank you for being there
whenever I need you.
When a friend lets me down
and I feel lonely,
touch me with your love.
Make me a good friend to my friends
so that we can always be there
for each other.
Amen

Song: 'Brother, sister, let me serve you' (CH4 694)

Friends and enemies:

Do you ever think of someone as an enemy? Maybe somebody who hurt you or did something mean to you.

Sometimes we might think of people who are somehow different from us as 'enemies', even when we don't really know them, or haven't even met them yet.

It's important to remember that 'enemy' is a very strong word – and it's really important to hear what Jesus said:

What else did Jesus say?:

'You have heard it said, "You shall love your neighbour and hate your enemy." But I say to you: Love your enemies and pray for those who hurt you, so that you may be children of God.' (Matthew 5:43–45)

Love your enemies … that's about the hardest thing Jesus ever said.

Even Jesus' close friends thought this was a bit too much. Just listen to a conversation between Jesus and his friend Peter:

Jesus and Peter (on friends and enemies):

Peter: Jesus?

Jesus: Yes, Peter?

Peter: I'm confused.

Jesus: Again, Peter?

Peter: It's about friends and enemies.

Jesus: Yes, Peter. What about friends and enemies?

Peter: I'm not sure who's who any more.

Jesus: Does it matter, Peter? Do you need some enemies?

Peter: Not really. I already seem to have more than a few.

Jesus: For example?

Peter: The Roman soldiers. They can stop us any time they like – for no good reason! Make us carry their packs for a mile along the road. Just like that. Doesn't matter where we're going. And with no thanks at all. I hate it. They have so much power, it's just not fair. And then there's that tax collector. You know, the really short one. He cheated us the other day. He's an enemy too.

Jesus: Peter, do you remember what I said about soldiers?

Peter: *(sighs ...)* Don't carry the pack for just one mile. Carry it for two.

Jesus: Right. Turn an enemy into a friend by showing a little generosity. A little kindness.

Peter: A little craziness, if you ask me.

Jesus: It's not crazy. It's love.

Peter: *(firmly)* Well, it won't work!

Jesus: Have you tried it?

Peter: … Uh … No. Not yet.

Jesus: Well, now's your chance. That short tax collector. His name's Zacchaeus. He's invited us to his house for tea.

Peter: Oh no. We're not going to eat with him and his friends?!

Jesus: Yes, we are.

Peter: But Jesus! People will talk. They'll say we mix with the wrong kind of people.

Jesus: Peter, just remember. The 'wrong kind of people' need the right kind of friends.

Peter: Friends like us, I suppose?

Jesus: Yes indeed. Friends who will take them just the way God made them!

Leader: Love your enemies … That's what Jesus said. Because Jesus knew what love can do to change our hearts. And help us become friends … Listen to a day in Jesus' life:

The story of Zacchaeus, a man changed in friendship (Luke 19):

Now Zacchaeus was a man who took tax money from people.

Tax money was what people had to pay their king to run the country.

But Zacchaeus often took more money from people than he was supposed to. He kept the extra money to make himself rich.

And so nobody liked him.

One day, Jesus was passing through the town where Zacchaeus worked.

Everyone went out to see Jesus, including Zacchaeus.

But Zacchaeus had a problem.

He was very short. So he couldn't see Jesus with everyone in front of him.

But he had an idea!

He ran ahead of the people and climbed a tall tree.

There he had the perfect place to watch Jesus coming along the road.

So when Jesus got to that tree, he stopped and looked up.

'Zacchaeus,' he said, 'come down right away! I need to stay at your house today.'

Zacchaeus scrambled down the tree. Imagine! Jesus wanted to stay with him!

Others around weren't too happy.

'Why would Jesus stay with a man who has cheated us on our taxes?' they grumbled.

But Zacchaeus was so glad to meet Jesus, he said, 'Lord, I want to do what is right. If I've cheated anyone, I'll pay them back four times what I owe them. And I'll sell half of what I own and give the money to the poor.'

Jesus was very pleased Zacchaeus had chosen to do the right thing.

'Zacchaeus, today you are a friend of God!'

Zacchaeus became a friend of God that day, an *amigo de Cristo*.

Even though Zacchaeus had done some mean things and cheated people, Jesus changed his heart by treating Zacchaeus like a friend.

Friends of the Lord really try to turn enemies into friends by never giving up on people like Zacchaeus who need some love in their lives.

Let's sing the chorus of 'Amigos de Cristo' again!

Song: 'Amigos de Cristo'

Offering

Friendship bracelets:

A friendship bracelet lets you know somebody thinks of you as a friend. You get a nice feeling from a friendship bracelet. Our *(youth group, etc)* made friendship bracelets for us to share today. If you need to know you are a friend of the Lord, keep it and wear it yourself. When someone asks about it, tell them you're an *'amigo de Cristo'*. But if you have a good friend, you could give them this bracelet so they'll remember they have a good friend in you, and have a good feeling, and remember you every time they see the bracelet.

So let's hand out the bracelets – make sure everyone gets one – so we'll all remember we're friends of the Lord!

(Play music during this: any song about sharing God's love would be good.)

Praying for friends and family and everyone else:

Voice 1:	Now please hold on to a bead on your bracelet *(if the bracelets have beads)* as we pray: to help you think about someone in particular you want to pray for today *(pause)* ...
Leader:	Show us how to care for one another.
All:	**Make us good friends of the Lord.**

Voice 2:	God of love and loving, today we pray for all the people who matter to us: we pray for our friends – old and new, near and far, those who are dear to us and those who have disappointed us. May your love make our friendships stronger.
Leader:	Show us how to care for one another.
All:	**Make us good friends of the Lord.**

Voice 3:	We pray for the members of our families: those who live close to us, those who live far away and those we've lost touch with. Thank you for family members who encourage us and help us through hard times,

and we pray for anyone in our family
we find hard to understand
or to love or get along with.
May your love make our families stronger.

Leader: Show us how to care for one another.
All: **Make us good friends of the Lord.**

Voice 4:   We pray for our neighbours:
those we know and trust
and those who seem a little different or distant.
We pray for people we've considered enemies,
and for people around us who haven't mattered at all to us.
Help us see each person we know or think about
as someone you love and someone who should matter to us.
May your love make our love for all our neighbours stronger.

Leader: Show us how to care for one another.
All: **Make us good friends of the Lord.**

Leader: And we pray for ourselves –
help us see in ourselves all the things you love about us;
help us remember the things
that can make us good friends to others
and help us share all those gifts with the world.
So that everyone who meets us knows
that we are good friends of the Lord.
Amen

Closing song: 'We are one in the Spirit', by Peter Scholtes, in various songbooks

Blessing

Sources and acknowledgements:

This service includes a version of an original story by Dr Nancy Cocks, 'Fergie's Best Friend' © 1997; and a 'Jesus and Peter' sketch, on the model of those created by the Wild Goose Resource Group, by Nancy Cocks, from *Invisible We See You*, Wild Goose Publications, 2006.

Companions on the journey
A blessing of pets and animals who
are a part of our lives

Thom M Shuman

This service is suitable for use at any time but would be particularly good during the Season of Creation in September, or on 4th October to mark the Feast of Saint Francis of Assisi: friend, protector and patron saint of animals.

Opening sentences:

Yes! We will praise God!
We will praise God in dog-parks.
We will praise God in paddocks.

Yes! We will praise God!
We will praise God in our aquariums.
We will praise God from our perches.

A little boy with a purring cat on his lap,
a young girl teaching a puppy to roll over,
an old woman conversing with her pretty parrot,
an old man cleaning out the rabbit hutch –
let them all praise God's name!

Yes! We praise the God of all creatures!

Suggested Bible readings: Genesis 1:20–25; Genesis 9:14–15; Exodus 23:4–5; Psalm 84:1–4; Psalm 148; Matthew 21:1–5

Song: 'All things bright and beautiful' (CH4 137)

A story about a pet/animals who are a part of our lives, for example:

Cocoa the Wonder Dog

In July 2003, Cocoa the Wonder Dog came into our lives. This was a big step for us (some in the family would say a crazy step), since, being confirmed cat people, we had not really had a relationship with a dog. And, like decisions in many families, this was not a unanimous one.

But it has proven to be a wise choice. For during those long, difficult months of surgery, chemotherapy and hospital stays, which followed our son's diagnosis of Stage 4 cancer, we always had someone at home waiting for us – filled with unconditional love and never-ending hope. I always thought it was true with cats, but Cocoa reminded us that pets are visible signs of that invisible grace God fills us with in each and every moment of our lives.

And Cocoa got us out of the house, especially on those mornings when bed seemed so safe and warm, and on those evenings when all we wanted to do was to veg out in front of the TV. Cats are perfectly content to take care of their business, in their way and time, but dogs – especially a dog like Cocoa – demand to be walked! And so we did – through puddles; in August heat; shuffling through snow, and trying not to slip on the ice underneath – we walked and walked and walked ... And along the way – on starry nights and cloudy days, in times of uncertainty as well as faithfulness, with tears marring our vision and joy bubbling on our lips – God was at work in our lives with the gentle presence of the Holy Spirit, and the healing grace of Jesus Christ.

We have grown accustomed to the belief that healing comes through medication, medical teams, hospitals, wonder treatments. And it does happen that way. But healing also comes in quiet moments: in the gentle hand on a shoulder, in eating a meal prepared by a neighbour, in the prayers of a community of faith, in the silent moments of the night. All too often, however, we are not alert enough to these moments and ways in which the healing power of God is poured upon us.

God does healing work in many remarkable ways, and often through rather 'unremarkable' people, and sometimes, even through a 'dumb animal' like Cocoa.

Note: We had been looking for a dog on and off for months, when we discovered Cocoa. She was the first dog, in all that searching, who came and approached us, rather than our approaching her first. Not long ago, there was a story on the news about a study which showed that some dogs have a special 'sense' by which they are able to 'smell' cancer in a person. We adopted Cocoa about two months before our son was diagnosed with cancer, and probably at the time when it was 'growing' within him. Gives one pause.

Litany of blessing:

Puppies who think puddles are perfect for baths;
white-muzzlers who chase squirrels in their dreams;
rescuers searching tirelessly through toppled buildings;
companions guiding the sightless,
eyes in whose depths we see God,
soft mouths which open doors;
greeters at the end of dreich days –
ball-chasers and stick-fetchers who get us moving ...

For every lab and Lhasa apso,
for every border collie and sheepdog,
for every golden retriever and Great Dane,
for every furry, four-footed best friend:

we give you thanks,
One whose name spelled backwards is dog,
for those companions who shadow us through life;
and we lift their names to you for blessing in this moment:

(Names of dogs may be spoken aloud, or held in the silence of people's hearts...)

Canaries that sing carols at evensong;
finches that lullaby us in the morning;
budgies who talk our ears off;
cockatiels who whistle to catch our attention;
caiques whose eyes twinkle with mischief;
macaws thinking up new ways to trick us;
cockatoos that cling to us 24/7;
parrots with their imperial natures ...

For every squawk and tweet,
for every flitter and flutter,
for every feather which brushes our cheek with gentleness,
for every beak which nips us with grace:

we give you thanks,
God of six-winged seraphim,

for the birds who send our hearts soaring;
and we lift their names to you for blessing in this moment:

(Names of birds may be spoken aloud, or held in the silence of people's hearts ...)

Mamas who carry their babies to safety by the scruff of their neck;
seniors who sleep their days away;
frightened felines who hide in the smallest spaces;
lappers who purr grace into our depths;
kittens who stalk sunbeams across kitchen floors;
mousers who keep our barns and basements free of problems;
foot-warmers on bitter winter nights;
tree-climbers who thwart every rescue attempt ...

For every tiger and tabby, for every Manx and Maltese,
for every tortoiseshell, marmalade and Russian Blue,
for every loquacious Siamese and every soft-spoken Scottish fold,
for every short-hair, long-hair, no-hair and in between:

we give you thanks,
God of gentle contemplation and contentment,
for those feline friends who see us for who we are,
even in the shadows of our lives;
and we lift their names to you for blessing in this moment:

(Names of cats may be spoken aloud, or held in the silence of people's hearts ...)

Thoroughbreds moving gently through the morning mist;
Clydesdales with hearts bigger than the sky;
New Forest ponies with history coursing through their veins;
Appaloosas that carry us surefooted along trails;
Tennessee walkers that show us how to persevere;
Welsh cobs that provide joy for children with disabilities ...

For puddlers and plodders,
for racers and wild mustangs,
for ponies accepting carrots from children,
and for those who shake their manes
to show us who's really in charge:

we give you thanks,
God of plains and farmlands,
for horses who love and accept us;
and we lift their names to you for blessing in this moment:

(Names of horses may be spoken aloud, or held in the silence of people's hearts ...)

For gerbils which teach kids responsibility,
and remind us of the value of smaller spaces;
for hamsters which show us how to compost,
and whose variety reflects the rich diversity of creation;
for cottontails and flop-eared bunnies
whose curiosity knows no bounds;
for leopard geckos and bearded dragons
which show us that it is OK to take time to relax;
for garter snakes, corn snakes and kingsnakes,
for spiders, mice, rats and other critters
others abhor but we adore;
for tropical fish like neon tetras and harlequin rasboras,
for algae eaters, loaches and silvery minnows who drive cats crazy –
for the rich, rainbow variety of your creation
and all those we are given to love and care for by your grace,
we give you thanks, and lift their names to you:

(Names of pets and different animals may be spoken aloud, or held in the silence of people's hearts ...)

Blessing of pets:

Folk bring their pets forward to be blessed, or those doing the blessing move among the gathering offering words of love, hope and thanksgiving for these companions on the journey. Make sure children get to take part in the blessing.

Closing prayer:

Lord, make us instruments of your peace.
Where there is hatred, let us sow love;
where there is injury, pardon;
where there is doubt, faith;
where there is despair, hope;
where there is darkness, light;
and where there is sadness, joy.

O, Divine Master,
grant that we may not so much seek to be consoled as to console;
to be understood as to understand;
to be loved as to love.
For it is in giving that we receive;
it is in pardoning that we are pardoned;
it is in dying that we are born again
to eternal life.

– Saint Francis of Assisi

Note: 'Canticle of all creatures', by Saint Francis, would also be a good closing prayer. You might also like to tell a story about Saint Francis and his love for/connection with animals, e.g. 'Saint Francis preaching to the birds' (prayers and stories of St Francis available online).

Folk and animals leave as they wish. Or have a pet show in the church!

Sources and acknowledgements:

'Cocoa the Wonder Dog' – by Thom M. Shuman, from *Gathered and Scattered: Readings and Meditations from the Iona Community*, Neil Paynter (Ed.), Wild Goose Publications, 2007

'Prayer of St Francis', from *Iona Abbey Worship Book*, Wild Goose Publications, 2001

Hunger for justice

'What's for dinner tonight, mum?'

Nancy Cocks

Opening responses:

Leader: For a child in the UK, poverty is …
All: Not having friends for a sleepover.
Men: Getting ill because we can't afford to heat the house.
Women: Missing out on birthday parties because we can't afford a gift.
All: Not having a pet because it costs too much.

Leader: For a child in the UK, hunger and poverty is …
All: Going to school with no breakfast.
Men: Knowing mum has gone without food so we can eat.
Women: Pretending you have forgotten your lunch.
All: Going to bed hungry.

Leader: For a child in the UK, being poor in the midst of plenty is …
All: Hearing mum and dad fighting about money.
Women: Not being able to have new clothes or shoes.
Men: Never going on holiday.
All: Having food from a food bank.[1]

Note: adapt the above responses to your own country, for example:

Leader: For a Canadian child, poverty is …
All: Getting a Christmas hamper from the Salvation Army.
Men: Feeling ashamed when my dad can't get a job.
Women: Not getting to go to birthday parties.
All: Not ever getting a pet because it costs too much.

Leader: For a Canadian child, hunger and poverty mean …
All: Not getting pizza on pizza day at school.
Men: Not getting a hot dog on hot dog day.
Women: Pretending you forgot your lunch.
All: Not having any breakfast sometimes.

Leader: For a Canadian child, being poor in the midst of plenty means …
All: Not getting to go on school trips.
Men: Not being able to go to Cubs or play soccer.
Women: Not being able to have your friends sleep over.
All: Hearing mom and dad fight over money.[2]

Song

First reading: 1 Kings 17:1, 8–13a

Meet Pancake Boy … (based on 1 Kings 17:8–16):

'What's for supper tonight, mum?'

I *know* what she's going to say: 'Pancakes.'

What else can you make from a jar of flour and a jug of oil?

You might think a kid like me would look forward to pancakes.

But just imagine having pancakes every night for a month!

And then imagine having pancakes every morning and every night for six months.

Multiply that by ten and you'll get the picture.

Even before that crazy prophet named Elijah showed up, we'd been eating pancakes every meal for what seemed like years!

That's what it's like when there isn't much to go around.

I was actually glad when that stranger came to our door and asked to be fed. At last! I thought. We'll get something more than pancakes.

Mum can't give a guest the last bit of our oil and flour, I thought.

I thought for sure she'd have something tucked away, a treat for my birthday maybe. But no, all we had in the house was oil and flour.

She was scared to give the last bit away. Thought I'd starve.

Ha! That might be better than pancakes forever and ever, amen!

The thing I hate about this famine – and being this poor in a famine – is that I don't get any choice about anything. Pancakes, pancakes, pancakes.

No syrup, no sausage, just pancakes.

That stranger seemed mighty glad to have pancakes.

He assured my mother we wouldn't run out of stuff if we shared our oil and flour with him.

I can still remember his words:

'Thus says the Lord God of Israel: the jar of flour will not be emptied and the jug of oil will not fail until the day that the Lord sends rain on the earth.'

I don't know about you but I wish the Lord could send something better than rain – something better than pancakes!

Lord God of Israel, how about a little pizza for a growing boy?

'Hey, mum! What's for dinner tonight?' …

(A faraway voice shouts: 'Pancakes!')

Like I said – pancakes!

Chant: 'God bless to us our bread', John L. Bell, *Love and Anger*, Wild Goose Publications, or 'Dayeinu', Stainer & Bell

Second reading: John 6:1–9

Meet Sardine Boy … **(based on John 6:1–14):**

I can hardly wait to ask her 'What's for dinner tonight, mum?'

It's a little too soon. She's pretty mad at me right now. Can't figure out why I gave my lunch away today.

(Mimicking his mother's voice:) 'I spent my hard-earned money on those sardines! I got up at 5am to bake that bread with my own hands. And you gave it to a perfect stranger. You ungrateful little boy.'

She wasn't there with me.

He did seem like a perfect stranger, that rabbi. I could see him roll his eyes when his friends couldn't think of a thing to do.

He'd been telling us some great stories but he could see we all needed some lunch and a bit of a break. He asked his friends to get things organised but those guys had no clue. They were panicking. The guy named Philip was the worst.

(Mimicking an adult male voice:) 'Six months' wages wouldn't buy enough bread for everyone here to get a little.'

That was his idea. Send somebody back to town to pick up sandwiches. For a thousand or two! Yeah, right.

The rabbi just shook his head.

Now I had my lunch with me: five barley buns and two sardines. Mum won't let me go for a day without taking lunch along.

So I took it out of my sack and showed it to a guy named Andrew. I thought if I shared mine, others might join in. After all, no mother takes her kids for a day in the mountains without bringing along some lunch!

So the rabbi got us organised, sat us down, started passing my lunch around.

Sure enough, bread and fish came out of nowhere. There might have been some cheese and olives too, and a few oranges. Everybody got something to eat, for sure.

But then a really strange thing happened.

The rabbi said, 'Gather up the leftovers!' You should have seen the look on Philip's face. He thought the rabbi was crazy!

But they passed around some baskets and the baskets came back full. Then that rabbi, I think his name is Jesus, he gave me a bunch of leftovers to take home.

I know when I ask mum what's for dinner, she's going to give me a hard time.

(Mimicking again:) 'I gave you the last two fish in the pantry, you wasteful boy.'

And then I'm going to bring out my basket of leftovers. It will be a feast! Sardines for sure, but some cheese and olives too. Amazing what happens when people share their lunch!

(Calling:) 'Hey, mum! What's for dinner tonight?' ...

Chant: 'God bless to us our bread' or 'Dayeinu'

Symbolic action:

Use felt markers to fill a paper plate with God's abundance, to draw and colour in a full healthy plate of food – veggies, meat, grains, fruit, ice cream: create the kind of dinner you'd like to serve every hungry child tonight.

Then pin your plate on a noticeboard: as an act of prayer that every child in your community, in the world will soon have their share of God's abundance. Think about what you can do to help those in your community, in the world who are hungry ... Pick up an action sheet/leaflet from the table *(e.g. from Christian Aid, Church Action on Poverty, Feed the Children ...)* and take it away with you.

Prayer:

Voice one: God our Maker, you made the world in all its goodness to give what each of your creatures needs to live.

The world offers us a feast of good things, flavours that please us and food to give us strength to work and play.

Thank you, God, for all the tables we gather around to enjoy good food from the good earth with family and friends.

Help us enjoy each mouthful and each meal. These are precious gifts!

Voice two: God of Life, the miracles in the Bible show us how goodness grows in the world when people share your gifts of food.

We pray for all those people who have to worry about where their next meal comes from, for parents who would like to serve more but just can't afford it, and for children who wish they could have another helping.

God, teach us to share the food we have so the hungry will have enough.

Voice one: God of Love, we thank you for everyone who shares what they have with someone in need. And we pray for everyone who reaches out for help. May they meet kindness and respect in those with something to share.

Voice two: God of Hope, we pray for those who lead our communities and our country. Help them figure out how to help the hungry so they can have enough to eat every day.

Voice one: As we pray together for our daily bread, make us hungry for justice that will share the bread as Jesus hoped:

Lord's Prayer (said together)[3]

Song: 'For the crowd of thousands', words by Fred Kaan, Hope Publishing

Closing prayer:

Lord, to those who are hungry,
give bread.
And to those who have bread,
give a hunger for justice.

Latin American prayer

Sources and acknowledgements:

1. Responses adapted by Nancy Cocks from ecumenical material prepared for the International Day for the Eradication of Poverty, and by Rachel McCann from material by the Child Poverty Action Group, www.cpag.org.uk

2. Responses adapted by Nancy Cocks from ecumenical material prepared for the International Day for the Eradication of Poverty

3. These prayers were adapted and simplified from material published by the Canadian Food Grains Bank in Faith: *As If Food Matters*. This excellent resource on food issues is available as a free download through the website of CFGB: foodgrainsbank.ca

What is valuable and true
A liturgy for economic witness

Norman Shanks

Gathering:

God of the cosmos, God of the commonplace,
THROUGH YOUR GRACE WE SEEK TO DO WHAT IS REQUIRED OF US.

God of the mundane, God of mystery,
THROUGH YOUR GRACE WE SEEK TO DO JUSTICE.

God-in-the-midst, God on the margins,
THROUGH YOUR GRACE WE SEEK TO LOVE KINDNESS.

God of power and plenty, God of the dispossessed,
THROUGH YOUR GRACE WE SEEK TO WALK HUMBLY IN YOUR WAY.

Song: 'God of freedom, God of justice' (CH4 263)

Prayer:

God of freedom and justice,
God of grace and truth,
in the glory of earth, sea and stars,
in the kaleidoscope of human experience,
we celebrate your loving kindness.

Forgive us when we stray from your way
and ignore the potential of your grace to bring new life and light
into the darkest place,
the most difficult situation.
Forgive the sins and suffering of our society
in which we are complicit.
Set us free from the prison of grudging hearts,
mean desires, vain ambitions,
resentful or envious spirits;
give us the courage in all things, at all times,
to act with compassion, justice and generosity,
through Jesus Christ, our Lord.
Amen

Contemporary adaptation of Psalm 72:

GIVE TO YOUR LEADERS GOOD JUDGEMENT, O GOD,
AND A SENSE OF WHAT IS RIGHT.

A: May they govern your people with justice
and do right for those who are powerless.

B: May the mountains bring peace for the people,
and the hills bring forth justice.

A: May they defend the poor among the people,
save the children of those who are needy,
and crush the oppressor.

B: May they endure as long as the sun,
like the moon through all generations;

A: Like the rains that fall on the early crops,
like the showers that water the earth.

B: May justice flower in their days,
and peace till the moon is no more.

A: May they rule from sea to sea,
and from the river to the ends of the earth.

B: May they rescue the needy when they cry out,
and the poor who have no one to help them.

A: May they have pity on the weak and powerless;
may they save the lives of the poor.

B: May they redeem them from oppression and violence,
and regard their blood as precious.

A: To them, long life and continuous prayers
as, day by day, they are blessed.

B: Let grain be abundant throughout their land,
and wave on the tops of the mountains.

A: Let the crops blossom like Lebanon
and the people flourish in the cities
like the grass of the fields.

B: Blessed be their name for ever;
may their names last as long as the sun.
In them let all the nations be blessed;
and proclaim their happiness.

BLESSED BE GOD, THE GOD OF THE FAITHFUL PEOPLE,
WHO ALONE DOES WONDROUS DEEDS.
BLESSED FOR EVER BE THE GLORIOUS NAME OF GOD.
MAY THE WHOLE EARTH BE FILLED WITH GOD'S GLORY!
AMEN! AMEN!

Iona Abbey Worship Book

Song: 'O Lord, all the world belongs to you', from *Songs of God's People* (84)

Bible readings: e.g. Isaiah 58:1–9, St Luke 16:19–31

Litany:

A: Poverty and inequality are a blot on any society that claims to be civilised and compassionate.

B: Blessed are the poor, for theirs is the kingdom of God … Blessed are those who hunger and thirst for justice, for they shall be filled *(St Luke 6:20, St Matthew 5:6)*.

A: The gap between the richest and the least well-off in Britain is still widening – an unequal society is an unhappy and unhealthy society.

B: The Gospel tells us that Jesus proclaimed fullness of life for all: 'I came that they may have life, and have it abundantly' *(St John 10:10)*.

A: It is a scandal that 'CEOs earn 331 times more than average workers, 774 times more than minimum wage earners' *(AFL-CIO PayWatch, 2014)*.

B: They have grown fat and sleek. They know no limits in deeds of wickedness ... and they do not defend the rights of the needy *(Jeremiah 5:28)*.

A: Woe to those who pursue policies of austerity and welfare reform that work against the common good and increase the suffering and vulnerability of many.

B: God knows how great are the sins of those who afflict the righteous and push aside the needy *(Amos 5:12)*.

A: Woe to bankers' bonuses and the bedroom tax.

B: It is easier for a camel to go through the eye of a needle than for someone who is rich to enter the kingdom of God *(St Luke 18:25)*.

A: Woe to all policies that render benefits-claimants and asylum-seekers destitute.

B: Let justice roll down like waters, and righteousness like an ever-flowing stream *(Amos 5:24)*.

A: Woe to the culture of performance-related pay, the dominance of the values of the marketplace and those who place targets and measurement above the quality of caring.

B: What does God require of us? – to do justice, to love kindness and to walk humbly with God *(Micah 6:8)*.

A: Blessed are those who expose the myths and lies about those who are poor.

B: Cease to do evil, learn to do good; seek justice, rescue the oppressed, defend the orphan, plead for the widow *(Isaiah 1:16–17)*.

A: Blessed are those who seek tax justice and stand in solidarity with those on the margins.

B: The house of the wicked is destroyed, but the tent of the upright flourishes *(Proverbs 14:11)*.

A: Blessed are those who strive for a living wage and food justice.

B: Since there will never cease to be some in need on the earth, I therefore command you, 'Open your hand to the poor and needy neighbour in your land' *(Deuteronomy 15:11).*

A: Blessed be God – source of all generosity and grace, all justice and joy.

B: God is our refuge and strength, a very present help in trouble ... Praise God whose steadfast love endures for ever *(Psalm 46:1; Psalm 136:26).*

Action:

Depending on location, etc: candle-lighting, as folk reflect on issues, groups or individuals they are concerned about. Or designate particular areas of the church, or other venue, for example: Tax Haven, Top Bankers' Club, Shopping Mall, Job Centre, Payday Loan Shop, etc, and invite people to come and 'occupy' these areas to protest against injustice; or designate areas, for example: Church Action on Poverty, Poverty Truth Commission, Poverty Alliance, Child Poverty Action Group ... and invite people to come and express their solidarity, take away campaign leaflets, etc.

Prayer:

God, meet us in the silence –
the place beyond the business and the bustle,
the chatter and the clutter,
beyond our preoccupations and prejudices.

There bless us with wisdom, insight and vision
to discern and lay hold of what is valuable and true,
to glimpse, hope and strive for possibilities of transformation
and fulfilment,
to commit ourselves to the new future
in which you are calling us to share.

Silence

Lord Jesus Christ,
in your earthly life you failed to live up to people's expectations.
Faced with testing situations, you were outrageously inventive.
In human relationships you were outrageously imaginative,
compassionate and straight-speaking.
Your love for the poor showed you to be
outrageously committed to justice.
You lacked balance, perhaps were short of diplomatic skills;
yet you are the way, the truth, the life.
It is human expectations that need to be changed.
So make us unbalanced, we pray –
not saying on the one hand, on the other to excuse inaction;
not pandering to social prejudices;
willing to jettison advancement, prestige
in favour of truthful living;
prepared to spend our lives sacrificially
to share in the building of God's kingdom
and the doing of God's will on earth,
for we want to follow in your footsteps.

Living God, may the mind of Christ be ours;
clothe us with your grace and grittiness,
help us to embody the vision and values of your kingdom
and be ready to face whatever may come
as we seek to do your will.
In Jesus' name we pray.
Amen

(Inspired by a prayer by Ian M. Fraser)

Song: 'Sing we a song of high revolt', from *Songs of God's People* (96)

Closing responses:

In our concerns and in our choices
GOD IS WITH US.

In our disappointments and in our joys
GOD IS WITH US.

In our protesting and in our serving
GOD IS WITH US.

Now and always
GOD IS WITH US.

God of the tipping point
A service of sorrowing, defiance and commitment

Alison Swinfen

Adapted from worship in Iona Abbey during the Iona Community's summer Community Week, 2015.

For this service you will need a set of scales with a balancing basket and counterweights (other types of scales might work too). Test all this out beforehand (see action).

Give each person a small stone or a feather as they come in.

Welcome

Opening responses:

Jesus says, 'I am the Way for you.'
AND SO WE COME TO FOLLOW CHRIST.

Jesus says, 'I am the Truth for you.'
AND SO WE COME TO DWELL IN THE LIGHT.

Jesus says, 'I am the Life for you.'
AND SO WE COME,
LEAVING BEHIND ALL ELSE TO WHICH WE CLING.[1]

Song: 'Don't tell me of a faith that fears/the sorrow', from *Love and Anger* or *Enemy of Apathy*, John L. Bell and Graham Maule, Wild Goose Publications

Scripture: Lamentations 1:16–22

Reflection:

Voice 1:

Who did this? There is an eerie calm as the bulldozers move in and begin to destroy the home. The family stand around outside watching as their walls fall in, and the teacups, hastily left on the table, fall to the floor, as if in slow motion. Next to them: witnesses, neighbours, peace accompaniers, a journalist, writing. Who did this?

Voice 2:

Who did this? The bedroom is empty but all her possessions are still there. She has fled in the clothes she was standing up in. In the home, anger subsiding, a father begins to wipe the floor of the mess. Who did this?

Voice 3:

Who did this? The redundancy pools have been created and the letters have gone out. The names of those to lose their jobs are now known, as are the names of those spared, this time. The union's efforts are to no avail.

Leader:

Who did this? O Lamentation. Who will stop my pain?

Voice 1:

Who did this to Jerusalem – split into sections, riven with strife, settlers' houses built onto the homes of Palestinians. Who did this? Such a great city. So much history, so much to offer. Who did this?

Voice 2:

Who allowed this to happen? She is such a lovely girl, so full of potential, life, hope. So much to offer. Who would do such a thing?

Voice 3:

Who did this to our work? Took an axe to the best programme – after all that effort of building it up into something we could be so proud of, against all the odds. Look at us now. Shame on them. Who did this?

Leader:

O Lamentation. Would that I had never lived to see such a thing, to witness such a thing, such a terrible, terrible thing. Where are you, O my God? Where is your kingdom now? Woe to those who caused me such shame. O Lamentation …

Silence

Song: 'Lo, I am with you', from *There Is One Among Us*, John L. Bell, Wild Goose Publications

Bible reading: Luke 18:1–8 (The parable of the persistent widow)

Invitation to commitment:

Margaret Legum, an economist from South Africa and member of the Iona Community, used to often describe the struggle against apartheid as *'like a rhino on a seesaw being attacked by gnats'*. At first the rhino wasn't bothered but, as the number of gnats increased, eventually it moved off, and the scales tipped … Like the image of snowflakes falling steadily and piling on a branch which, one day, finally snaps … or the persistent widow in Jesus' parable, in which we imagine and hope for a dramatic change in favour of the poor and oppressed.

In a moment I will invite you to come and make a sign of commitment to this struggle for justice, this work of defiant grief, born of lamentation, born of hope. As there is no ready supply of rhinos here and midges are notoriously hard to control, I'm instead going to invite you to come and add a *(stone/feather)* to the scale, in the hope of reaching a tipping point: a tipping point in favour of the poor and oppressed of the world …

But first, let us pray:

Voice 4:

Prayer:

God of the tipping point,
do not lead us into naivety.
Do not countenance a lazy complacency.
Do not nurture in us false optimism,
or self-congratulation.
For the weapons are proliferating;
and the nuclear abomination remains;

and children live in deepening poverty;
the homeless and destitute are many;
and so many have turned away from your ways
and curse your name.
The leaders say to refugees and asylum seekers:
'You are not welcome here.'
'Let them drown', and governments
work against the offer of refuge, sanctuary and a home.
Injustice is manufactured, purchased,
installed at the checkpoints,
and feared.
And the world's profiteers rule.

But take this as a humble sign
that we defy those who say,
'There is no alternative.'
Following instead your command to be wise as serpents
and innocent as doves,
still holding to your strange hope;
and committing anew to the vulnerable agony
of sharing in your compassion.
Amen

Symbolic action:

Leader:

I invite you now to come up and add your *(stone/feather)*, as a symbol of
the hope of achieving a tipping point.

Song: 'Lo I am with you' *(as people make a sign and commitment up to the tipping point)*

Affirmation from South Africa:

It is not true that this world and its inhabitants are doomed to die and be lost; THIS IS TRUE: FOR GOD SO LOVED THE WORLD THAT HE GAVE HIS ONLY SON SO THAT EVERYONE WHO BELIEVES IN HIM SHALL NOT DIE, BUT HAVE EVERLASTING LIFE.

It is not true that we must accept inhumanity and discrimination, hunger and poverty, death and destruction; THIS IS TRUE: I HAVE COME THAT THEY MAY HAVE LIFE, AND HAVE IT ABUNDANTLY.

It is not true that violence and hatred shall have the last word, and that war and destruction have come to stay for ever; THIS IS TRUE: FOR TO US A CHILD IS BORN, TO US A SON IS GIVEN, IN WHOM AUTHORITY WILL REST, AND WHOSE NAME WILL BE PRINCE OF PEACE.

It is not true that we are simply victims of the powers of evil that seek to rule the world; THIS IS TRUE: TO ME IS GIVEN AUTHORITY IN HEAVEN AND ON EARTH, AND LO, I AM WITH YOU ALWAYS, TO THE END OF THE WORLD.

It is not true that we have to wait for those who are specially gifted, who are the prophets of the church, before we can do anything; THIS IS TRUE: I WILL POUR OUT MY SPIRIT ON ALL PEOPLE, AND YOUR SONS AND DAUGHTERS SHALL PROPHESY, YOUR YOUNG PEOPLE SHALL SEE VISIONS, AND YOUR OLD FOLK SHALL DREAM DREAMS.

It is not true that our dreams of liberation of humankind, our dreams of justice, of human dignity, of peace, are not meant for this earth and its history; THIS IS TRUE: THE HOUR COMES, AND IT IS NOW, THAT TRUE WORSHIPPERS SHALL WORSHIP GOD IN SPIRIT AND IN TRUTH.[2]

Closing responses:

Look at your hands, see the touch and the tenderness,
GOD'S OWN FOR THE WORLD.

Look at your feet, see the path and the direction,
GOD'S OWN FOR THE WORLD.

Look at your heart, see the fire and the love,
GOD'S OWN FOR THE WORLD.

Look at the cross, see God's Son and our Saviour,
GOD'S OWN FOR THE WORLD.

This is God's world,
AND WE WILL SERVE GOD IN IT.[3]

Song

Blessing

Sources and acknowledgements:

1. Opening responses, from *Iona Abbey Worship Book*, Wild Goose Publications, 2001 © Iona Community

2. Affirmation from South Africa, taken from *Iona Abbey Worship Book*, Wild Goose Publications, 2001, by Allan Boesak ©

3. Closing responses, from *Iona Abbey Worship Book*, Wild Goose Publications, 2001 © Iona Community

A framework for
a memorial event

Tom Gordon

Purpose

The primary purposes of a memorial event are to allow people, in a corporate setting, to remember loved ones, to have their loss recognised, and to find that their sorrow and their journey of bereavement has echoes of other people's experiences. It should not be seen either as an attempt to solve or diminish grief, or as a be-all-and-end-all of bereavement support.

Content and style

The framework, delivery and content of a memorial event should always be determined by the context and circumstances of the people involved. Consequently, the event should be inclusive, and the language, music and readings used should be accessible to all. The setting should be one of warmth and welcome, and the delivery of the event should be simple and straightforward. In general terms, the event should not be overlong. The framework of the event should be clear, and the framework which follows indicates that a beginning – a recognition of the reality of grief – a middle – concentrating on an act of remembrance – and an ending – offering hope and purpose for the future – is a useful model.

Religious or not?

The setting and purpose of the event will largely determine whether religious aspects are included or not. If it takes place in a church, for example, that will offer a clear signal to all who come that some religious aspects, such as the singing of a hymn, or the pronouncement of a blessing, might be included. However, two things should be noted: Firstly, a memorial event should not be seen as an opportunity to proselytise, as, despite the setting, there will be those attending who will feel alienated if religious certainties predominate. Secondly, even if the event has a religious context, the readings and music should not be confined to an exclusively religious resource base. The most important thing is that the event is inclusive. If the content, therefore, is handled sensitively, people will be able to take from the event the comfort and support they need.

Music

If music is used, pieces played should be short, appropriate and varied, as different styles of music will touch people in different ways. Using music gives people an opportunity to reflect and be comfortable with their own thoughts and remembrances, and permits them to process their issues of loss in their own way and not always as directed by the spoken words. It is useful to include at least one piece of music with words, as many modern songs have lyrics of extraordinary depth and meaning. Like all music used, this should always be accessible to the people involved, and the context will determine what is appropriate. Where a song is played, the words should be printed and in people's hands so that they can follow them themselves, as the lyrics of songs are not always understood on a first hearing. Copyright permission should be looked at carefully. (The music designated in the framework here is for guidance purposes only, but is included to illustrate what might be possible.)

Readings

Readings should be short and the language and style appropriate to the context of the event. If possible, they should be printed and in people's hands so that they can be followed while they are being offered, and to allow people the opportunity to take them away and reflect on them when the event is over. Again, copyright issues should be carefully handled. It is always useful to have more than one voice involved with the event, and to have a mixture of male and female voices. The readings should always be read clearly so that they are heard and understood by all the participants.

A memorial action

As well as utilising appropriate words and music, it is important that the event includes an activity which is focused on remembrance in which all participants can be involved. Again, the style of this will be determined by the context of the event and the needs of the people attending. But the memorial action should be distinctive and physical, i.e. it should involve some movement and action for the participants. Such an action might be the writing of the name of the loved one to be remembered on a card and the participant coming forward to place the name on the altar or table. It could be the lighting of a candle; the placing of a flower in a display; the use of a pebble: either taking one away to remember a loved one, or placing a pebble in a bowl of remembrance. There are many possibilities, but people will need something which is a specific act of remembrance. The use of music is appropriate here, but silence is also an important and useful tool.

Following the event

There should be an opportunity for people to stay and chat after the event is over. A cup of tea is always useful; and it is helpful to have people around who can engage with those who may be finding things difficult. Equally, there may be those who wish to slip away and talk with no one, and their wishes should always be respected.

The framework

What follows is an event which lasts about half an hour, including music. The content in this case is non-religious, and is an attempt to be inclusive to all who participate. The readings, if utilised, may require copyright permission, but the 'linking script', i.e. the framework of the event, and the reflections written by me require no additional copyright clearance.

The complete event is a revised version of one of three such events offered annually as part of the bereavement support service in the Marie Curie Hospice, Edinburgh.

Tom Gordon

Section 1: Introduction

The setting: People attending should be welcomed, given a clear indication of where to go and what to expect, and provided with the necessary information (order of service, leaflet of readings, etc) to guide them through what is to take place. It is important to have suitable music playing while people gather.

Music (for gathering): 2nd movement of Mozart's Clarinet Concerto

Leader: Introduction and welcome: explain who is to be involved; the format of the event; and, if necessary, the reasons for having a memorial event; explain timings; invite people to stay for tea afterwards, etc.

Section 2: The rightness of grieving

Leader:

As people try their best to move through their bereavement journey, sometimes they are embarrassed by their grief when they are offered support. And so they respond with statements such as:

'I should be coping better than this.'

'I'm sorry for bothering you with my sadness.'

'I promised myself I wouldn't break down.'

'I ended up in tears in Tesco.'

'This isn't the way I expected it to be.'

And yet we know, and you know too, that it's right to grieve
and it's good to express our sorrow.
If our feelings are honest and true,
then it's OK to acknowledge they're there.

And, even more than that,
we need people who will allow us to be as we are
and as we need to be,
who will accept our tears
and not give us a hard time.

Some years ago, a widower,
whose wife had died after fifty-two years of marriage,
wrote this to a friend,
whose own wife had recently died:

Reader 1:

'I know you will be sad right now,
for I know well enough what that is like.
I wish I could say something clever
that would make your hurting go away.
But I can't.
It looks like we just have to hurt for a while, doesn't it?
And no one's going to make the sadness suddenly go away.
But, you know, I reckon it's all right to hurt …
And if someone understands that you're hurting,
it helps, that's for sure.
It's OK to cry.
I had to learn that.
So here's someone who'll share your tears.
Because I came to understand that
it's only through the tears

that you learn what it's really like to laugh.
And, even though you'll wonder
whether it's right to be happy when you think you should be down,
it's only after feeling sadness that you can know what joy is like.
So, allow yourself to feel what comes naturally –
if you cry, you cry …
and if you laugh, you laugh …
And I promise you this –
one day life will be easier,
and it will really be easier to smile.'

Tom Gordon, a former hospice chaplain, puts it this way:

Reader 2:

'Sometimes I collect pebbles from the shore near where I live.
The beach has pebbles of many sizes,
with different colours, from different rocks.
They were jagged once,
with sharp edges, and rough sides.
But now, over time,
with the movement of the waves and the grinding of the sand,
they are smoothed down, rounded and soft to the touch.
That's what time does to the sharpness of our grief:
what was once jagged and misshapen,
hard and painful to hold on to,
becomes smooth and rounded in our hands.'

Leader:

That's a helpful picture for many people.

So, to give us time to think about
the hurt becoming manageable
and the rough bits being smoothed
as we learn to live and smile again,
let's listen to a piece of music …

Music: 'El Noy de la Mare', from *Romantic Melodies for Guitar* by David Jaggs

Section 3: Beginning to move forwards

Leader:

So, when there are signs of laughter amidst the tears,
signs of pain and coping somehow mixing together –
of rough edges that hurt
becoming a smooth stone of remembrances,
then these are signs of moving forward ...
slowly, bit by bit, moving forward ...

Someone, whose name is now lost in the mists of time,
an anonymous writer, wrote this about that experience:

Reader 1:

When cherished ties are broken, the chain of life is shattered.

Yet, even in pain you are beginning to realise
that your beloved will never vanish,
and thoughts of your beloved will remain with you.
No one can take away your hurt,
because no one can take away your love.
Nothing can detract from the happiness you once shared.

Memory is a master painter –
lining indelible images upon your mind's canvas,
with reminiscences, both happy and sad.
As long as you live, so will your loved ones.
Memories bring strength and blessings.

The beauty of their lives is forever enshrined in your heart,
abiding as a lasting and loving benediction
in the unending circle of time.

Leader:

'In the unending circle of time' ...
Perhaps that's the clue:

that only time can hold the answer,
only time can offer healing and hope.

Poet Ann Thorpe, writing of her own sorrow, puts it this way:

Reader 2:

I have to believe that you still exist Somewhere
That you still watch me Sometimes
That you still love me Somehow.
I have to believe that life has meaning Somehow
That I am useful here Sometimes
That I make small differences Somewhere.
I have to believe that I need to stay here for Some time
That all this teaches me Something
So that I can meet you again Somewhere.

Leader:

Somehow …
Somewhere …
Somehow …
Sometime …
There is hope …
There is healing …
There is change …
There is beginning again …

As bereaved people reflect on what's happening to them,
here are the kinds of things they say.
Perhaps their words can speak for all of us:

Reader 1:

I am sorry I haven't got round to writing before now to thank you
for all you did for my family.
I did try writing several times but only ended up in tears.
Words are not enough to express our thanks for your support.

Reader 2:

The important thing in it all
was that there were people who were prepared to be there
when you needed them.
They didn't have to say much,
but it was good to know they were around.

Reader 1:

I met an old friend the other day I hadn't spoken to in years.
She's lost her husband too,
and, you know, it was so good talking with someone
who really knew how I felt.
We've promised that we'll meet up regularly
and talk some more.

Reader 2:

My sister and I went to a cousin's wedding last week.
I wasn't looking forward to it at all.
But, do you know, I actually enjoyed the day –
apart from a couple of wobbly moments –
and found myself smiling again
for what seemed to be the first time in ages and ages.

Reader 1:

I feel so silly sometimes, breaking down over trivial things.
But, then, it was only me and my wife
who knew how much these little things mattered.

Reader 2:

I've been promising myself I'd phone you.
But it's hard to pick up the phone
and tell someone you're not doing too well.
So I thought I'd write and tell you I wasn't doing too well –

but, actually, I think I'm doing better than I thought I was,
if you see what I mean.
At least I'm not crying as I'm writing this.
So there's a good sign.

Reader 1:

I think as it is a new year I will try to think positive
and look to the future.
It isn't easy, as you know,
but it's important to look forward.

Reader 2:

I might have moved along since we spoke,
but the sadness never goes away for long.
I do feel, however,
that I am beginning to find courage to get back into life
and begin to live again.
And my football team won on Saturday –
for the first time in ages –
so life isn't all bad!

Music: 'Gymnopedie No. 3' by Erik Satie

Section 4: It's good to share and to remember

Leader:

Sometime … you begin again,
and you are able then to make a memorial
to take your remembrances
and fit them into the life that is unfolding for you …

Another anonymous writer,
reflecting on their own death,
and on how they would like to be remembered,
puts it this way:

Reader 1:

When I am gone, fear not to say my name;
nor speak of me in hushed tones
as though it were a shame for one to die.
Let me figure in your daily task;
speak of my loves and hates,
remembering the laughter and the tears.
This way, I'll be forever in your memory.

Leader:

So, if they are forever in your memory,
in laughter and tears,
let's take some time to focus on that …

Time of quiet

Leader:

So now we will share in a simple act of remembrance *(to be explained)*. And while we share in this, we'll listen to a piece of music.

Music: 'Something for Jamie', from *Leaving Friday Harbour* by the Battle-field Band

Act of remembrance

Silence

Leader:

Just as there is a time to remember and give thanks,
a time of sorrow and a time to smile …
so we are reminded that
there's a time for everything …

Reader 2:

For every thing there is a season,
and a time for every purpose under heaven.
A time to be born and a time to die.
A time to plant and a time to reap.
A time to kill and a time to heal.
A time to break down and a time to build up again.
A time to weep and a time to laugh.
A time to mourn and a time to dance.
A time to cast away stones and a time to gather them together.
A time to embrace and a time to refrain from embracing.
A time to gain and a time to lose.
A time to keep and a time to throw away.
A time to tear and a time to mend.
A time to be silent and a time to speak.
A time of love and a time of hate.
A time for war and a time for peace.
So, for all of us, it's about time …

Music: 'Time after time' by Cyndi Lauper and Robert Hyman, sung by Eva Cassidy, from *Time after Time*

Silence

Leader:

For some people prayer is important.
For others, it's being with their deep thoughts that's important.
So, however you approach it,
let's pray,
or let's be with our own thoughts,
and in remembrance,
let's give thanks.

Leader:

When it's our time to face the frailty of life,
give us patience to wait and to watch with love.

When it's our time to be honest about our mortality,
give us insight not to draw back from what is real.

When it's our time to be cast low with the sorrow of loss,
give us understanding to know the value of tears.

When it's our time to wonder if we'll ever cope,
give us acceptance of the support of others.

When it's our time to hurt with the nagging pains of grief,
give us tolerance and openness to the healing touch.

When it's our time to lift our heads and look at the world again,
give us awareness to see and know what's good.

When it's our time to smile once more,
give us the capacity to know that hope has come.

When it's our time to take a faltering step into a new beginning,
give us the purpose to start afresh.

When it's our time to pause and remember,
give us a reassurance that love is not lost.

(Tom Gordon)

An alternative at this point might be:

Sometimes I need strength –
because the next step seems so hard.
Give me the purpose to go on when I feel so weary with trying.

Sometimes I lack patience –
when progress feels so slow.

Give me what's needed for the future
even when the future's hard to contemplate.

Sometimes I've got no courage –
when problems are all I see ahead.
Give me the will to go on and believe that an easier path
may be just around the corner.

Sometimes I don't have enough insight –
to trust the promise that it will come right.
Give me the wisdom to know that those who love and care
will not abandon me when times are hard.

Sometimes I need faith –
when I do not know what I believe.
Give me the openness to see
something in the mystery to keep me going.

Sometimes my sense of purpose fails me –
and even fellow travellers don't seem to understand.
Give me new trust in their companionship
so I can keep going a bit more.

Sometimes hope seems to have abandoned me –
the hope I needed to keep on going and know it won't be in vain.
Give me hope when I feel hopeless
so I don't feel overwhelmed any more.

Sometimes I've got too much time –
and I don't know whether to remember and be sad
or remember and be thankful.
Give me the right time with my memories,
to grieve,
to smile.

(Tom Gordon)

Section 5: Looking to the future

Leader:

Thank you for coming today ...
We hope this time of remembrance has been useful for you.
Take it, and fit it into all the other times, good and bad,
that make up your journey forward.
Remember it, and let it help you on your way.

And to help with that, we offer you this final reflection,
titled 'You are all around'.
And it helps us to realise
that our remembering is not confined to here and now,
but is something we carry with us into our future,
to build it into all that is yet to come:

Reader 1:

I saw you in the roses
when they bloomed in summer light.
I glimpsed you in our holy place,
embraced by candlelight.
I heard you in the music,
though there was no song being sung.
And I knew that you were near me once again.

Reader 2:

I smelt you in the perfume
of a random passer-by.
I found you in the sunset
when it filled the evening sky.
I sensed you sit beside me,
though I knew no reason why.
And I'm glad that you were near me once again.

Reader 1:

I saw you in the footsteps
stretching far across the sand.
I felt you in the woodland
as you gently touched my hand.
I held you on the hillside,
though the moment was unplanned.
In embracing, you were near me once again.

Reader 2:

I watched you in the gentle waves
that lapped our favourite shore.
I laughed out loud though waves would drown
my voice with awesome roar.
I sensed you would be waiting
when my key unlocked my door.
And I longed to have you near me once again.

Reader 1:

I felt you lie beside me
as I lay in restless sleep.
I heard your gentle sobbing
in the times I had to weep.
I knew you in the silence
which will still our secrets keep.
And thank God, my love, you're near me once again.

Reader 2:

I need you when I need you,
when I love you to be near.
I love you when I love you,
in my laughing and my tears.

I miss you, and to lose you from my living is my fear.
I want you to be near me,
how I need you to be near me,
in our love you will be near me,
and, thank God, you're ever near me,
when my joy gives way to pain.
Yes, my love, you're here, so near me, once again.

(Tom Gordon, from New Journeys Now Begin*)*

Reader 1:

Different ways ...
Different experiences ...
But one common remembrance.

Leader:

Thank you for sharing part of this day with us.
We hope that this time together has been a move for good
that will fit into the whole picture of your life.

Explain folk can stay for tea ... Tell folk to take their time leaving ... that people are around if they need them ...

Music (for leaving): 'The Ruby', from *The Ruby* by Aly Bain and Phil Cunningham

A liturgy for setting out
on a pilgrimage and
a prayer for the journey

David Coleman & Chris Polhill

In this liturgy include many readers.

Opening quote:

A pilgrimage is a journey whose destination is ultimately the same as that from which you set out: through it, you are asking God to show you your life, your home, your place, in a new light.

Call to worship:

God said: 'Leave your country, your family and your relatives, and go to the land that I will show you.' (Genesis 12:1)

Song or hymn

Opening responses:

The day is coming
when things will change.
THE DAY IS COMING WHEN WE WILL SET OUT.

The day is coming to cross the sea,
to touch the earth,
to plant a seed,
to trust … and not look back.
TO TRUST AND NOT LOOK BACK.

The day has come when Christ sets out.
THE DAY HAS COME FOR FOOD AND FRIENDSHIP.

The day has come
not to flee but to embrace;
not to escape but to welcome;
not to shut out but, in safety and in community,
to trust and not look back.
TO TRUST AND NOT LOOK BACK.

The discipline of letting go (Luke 9:57–62):

Along the way, someone said to Jesus, 'I'll go anywhere with you!' Jesus said, 'Foxes have dens, and birds have nests; but the Son of Man doesn't have a place to call his own.'

Jesus told someone else to come with him. But they said, 'Lord, let me wait until I bury my father.' Jesus answered, 'Let the dead take care of the dead; whilst you go and tell about God's kingdom.' Then someone said to Jesus, 'I want to go with you, Lord; but first let me go back and take care of things at home.' Jesus answered, 'Anyone who starts ploughing and keeps looking back isn't worth a thing to God's kingdom.'

Dreaming and not looking back:

Off the top of your head, in small groups, talk about:

- What you need to stop doing
- What the world needs to stop doing
- What you would like to get round to one day
- One thing which would make the world a better place
- A sign which would encourage you
- A sign which would encourage the world

Soon we will set out.
We will find our ways converge and come together
for no one can always travel alone.
Strangers will cross our path.
But so will angels.
And there's the risk.

Costs and rewards of walking Christ's way (Mark 10:30):

Jesus said: 'You can be sure that anyone who gives up home or brothers or sisters or mother or father or children or land for me and for the good news will be rewarded. In this world they will be given a hundred times as many houses and brothers and sisters and mothers and children and pieces of land, though they will also be ill-treated.'

Soon we will set out.
Not to escape our lives but to catch up with them.
Not to look back at where we have come from,
but, from that distance,
to look forward to where we are heading.
We will travel
in the well-worn footsteps
of centuries of pilgrims,
to find food for our journey
as companions of Christ.

So we take time now to consider a person/people alongside whom we might like to walk in prayer. For them, we give up some time, some effort, some space ...

Time for silent prayer

Prayer action:

Passing a stone or cross amongst the group while praying aloud for people or situations, ending with silence.

God, who brings us together,
re-member us and all we care for.
Add your prayer to ours –
for this land,
this world,
and our daily lives.
AMEN

Song or hymn

Meeting: practical preparation for travelling and sharing

Final gathering:

DOWNTRODDEN CHRIST,
AS WE SET OUT
IN SANDALS, BOOTS AND TRAINERS,
ON WHEELS, AND BORNE BY ANGELS,
BE OUR LEADER AND OUR GUIDE,
OUR BACK-MARKER AND OUR PATIENCE,
WITH EACH OTHER,
WITH EACH CREATURE,
WITH OURSELVES –
WITH GOD'S GOOD INTENT
ALL AROUND US
ON OUR WAY.
AMEN

Closing song or hymn

A prayer for the journey

Journeying with you, Creator God,
is to journey in your world,
full of marvels and such beauty.
To glimpse eternity in sky and sea,
to feel the earth and rock beneath my feet.

Journeying with you, brother Jesus,
is to journey with your friends.
To meet and travel a while together,
then part at the crossroads,
knowing you are with us all.

Journeying with you, Holy Spirit,
is to journey with the wind.
To move to your wild music
then try to sing your song
so others may hear.

(Chris Polhill)

About the authors

Tim Aldred is an associate member of the Iona Community. He has worked for international development charities for most of his career, and is currently Head of Policy and Research at the Fairtrade Foundation. He lives in Bromley with Sally and their two daughters.

Sarah Anderson studied literature at Oxford University and is a primary-school teacher. She and David McNeish live in Orkney and have three children.

Dave Broom is a teacher and a former member of the Iona Community's Resident Group on Iona, where he worked as Sacristan in 2012. He is the author of *The Cross in the Marketplace* (Wild Goose).

Nancy Cocks is a former Deputy Warden of Iona Abbey, after which she took up the post of professor at Atlantic School of Theology in Halifax, Nova Scotia. She currently serves as the minister of St John's Presbyterian Church in Medicine Hat, Alberta. Nancy is the author of several books, including *Invisible We See You* and *Growing Up With God* (Wild Goose).

David Coleman is an Iona Community member, a URC minister and a digital artist with wide experience of multimedia in a worship context. He runs the Facebook page 'Lectionary clips and hymns'.

Ian M Fraser has been a pastor-labourer in heavy industry, a parish minister, Warden of Scottish Churches House, an Executive Secretary of the World Council of Churches, and Dean and Head of the Department of Mission at Selly Oak Colleges, Birmingham. He is the author of many books, including *Strange Fire, The Way Ahead, A Storehouse of Kingdom Things* and *Reinventing Theology as the People's Work* (Wild Goose). Ian is one of the original members of the Iona Community who helped George MacLeod to rebuild 'the common life' and the Abbey buildings on the isle of Iona. Throughout his life Ian has travelled the world, alone and with his wife, Margaret, visiting basic Christian communities. He has walked alongside slum dwellers in India and Haiti; Nicaraguan and Cuban revolutionaries; priests, nuns and catechists facing arrest and/or death in Central and South America; and small farming and fishing communities in the Philippines.

Tom Gordon is a former hospice chaplain, storyteller and member of the Iona Community. He is the author of several books, including *Look Well to This Day: A year of daily reflections, A Blessing to Follow: Contemporary parables for living, Welcoming Each*

Wonder: More contemporary stories for reflection, and *With An Open Eye: Parables with meaning for today*. Two of his books are based specifically on his experience as a hospice chaplain: *A Need for Living: Signposts on the journey of life and beyond* and *New Journeys Now Begin: Learning on the path of grief and loss*.

John Harvey was a member, with his wife, Molly, of the Gorbals Group Ministry in the 1960s, and a parish minister in Gorbals, Govan, and Raploch in Stirling. He was Warden of Iona Abbey for five years in the 1970s, and Leader of the Iona Community from 1988 to 1995. He has been a member of the Iona Community since 1964.

Annie Heppenstall currently works as a tutor for the interfaith seminary One Spirit, volunteers as a mental health 'chaplain' with the NHS, mentors Bards following a Druid path and is an elected Area Minister for the Society of St Francis (an Anglican contemplative Order). She lives in the West Midlands, with her priest husband, Ray Gaston, has a degree and MA in Theology and Religious Studies and a delight in the Feminine Divine.

David McNeish has been a hospital doctor, a worship musician and a campaigner for the Citizens Advice Bureau. He is the minister at Milestone Community Church in Orkney, a member of the Iona Community and Chair of Orkney Pilgrimage: www.stmagnusway.com.

Joy Mead is a member of the Iona Community and the author of several books, including *The One Loaf, A Telling Place, Making Peace in Practice and Poetry, Where Are the Altars?* and *Words and Wonderings*. She leads creative writing groups, and has been involved in development education and justice and peace work.

Yvonne Morland is a poet, liturgist and member of the Iona Community.

Chris Polhill is a member of the Iona Community and one of the first women priests in the Church of England. She is the author of *Eggs and Ashes* (with Ruth Burgess), *A Pilgrim's Guide to Iona Abbey, A Heart for Creation* and *In the Mists on the Shoreline*. She and her husband, John, run the Reflection Gardens, which highlights the Christian spiritual journey and environmental issues.

Norman Shanks is a former Leader of the Iona Community.

Thom M Shuman is the author of *The Jesse Tree: Daily readings for Advent, Gobsmacked: Daily devotions for Advent* and *The Soft Petals of Grace: Communion liturgies and other resources* (Wild Goose) and is a contributor to many Wild Goose anthologies and downloads. He lives in Ohio and is an associate member of the Iona Community.

Jan Sutch Pickard is a poet, preacher and storyteller living on Mull. She is a former Warden of Iona Abbey and Ecumenical Accompanier in Palestine and Israel. Her books and many resources include *Out of Iona: Words from a crossroads of the world*, *Between High and Low Water: Sojourner songs* and *A Pocket Full of Crumbs* (Wild Goose).

Alison Swinfen is UNESCO Professor for Refugee Integration through languages and the arts and co-convener of Glasgow Refugee, Asylum and Migration Network at the University of Glasgow (https://gramnet.wordpress.com). She is a member of the Iona Community.

Brian Woodcock is a former Iona Abbey warden.

Wild Goose Publications is part of the Iona Community

- An ecumenical movement of men and women from different walks of life and different traditions in the Christian church
- Committed to the gospel of Jesus Christ, and to following where that leads, even into the unknown
- Engaged together, and with people of goodwill across the world, in acting, reflecting and praying for justice, peace and the integrity of creation
- Convinced that the inclusive community we seek must be embodied in the community we practise

Together with our staff, we are responsible for:

- Our islands residential centres of Iona Abbey, the MacLeod Centre on Iona, and Camas Adventure Centre on the Ross of Mull

and in Glasgow:

- The administration of the Community
- Our work with young people
- Our publishing house, Wild Goose Publications
- Our association in the revitalising of worship with the Wild Goose Resource Group

The Iona Community was founded in Glasgow in 1938 by George MacLeod, minister, visionary and prophetic witness for peace, in the context of the poverty and despair of the Depression. Its original task of rebuilding the monastic ruins of Iona Abbey became a sign of hopeful rebuilding of community in Scotland and beyond. Today, we are about 280 Members, mostly in Britain, and 1500 Associate Members, with 1400 Friends worldwide. Together and apart, 'we follow the light we have, and pray for more light'.

For information on the Iona Community contact:
The Iona Community, 21 Carlton Court,
Glasgow G5 9JP, UK. Phone: 0141 429 7281
e-mail: admin@iona.org.uk; web: www.iona.org.uk

For enquiries about visiting Iona, please contact:
Iona Abbey, Isle of Iona, Argyll PA76 6SN, UK. Phone: 01681 700404
e-mail: ionacomm@iona.org.uk

Wild Goose Publications, the publishing house of the Iona Community
established in the Celtic Christian tradition of Saint Columba, produces
books, e-books, CDs and digital downloads on:

- holistic spirituality
- social justice
- political and peace issues
- healing
- innovative approaches to worship
- song in worship, including the work of the Wild Goose
  Resource Group
- material for meditation and reflection

For more information:

Wild Goose Publications
The Iona Community
21 Carlton Court, Glasgow, G5 9JP, UK

Tel. +44 (0)141 429 7281
e-mail: admin@ionabooks.com

or visit our website at
www.ionabooks.com
for details of all our products and online sales